Just Say
OM!

Soren Gordhamer

ADAMS MEDIA CORPORATION
Avon, Massachusetts

In memory of Teru Imai for a life well lived.

Published by
Adams Media Corporation
57 Littlefield Street, Avon, MA 02322
www.adamsmedia.com

ISBN: 1-58062-549-5

Printed in Canada.

J I H G F E D C B A

Library of Congress Cataloging-in-Publication data
available upon request from the publisher.

This publication is designed to provide accurate and authoritative information with regard to
the subject matter covered. It is sold with the understanding that the publisher is not engaged
in rendering professional medical advice. If assistance is required, the services of a competent
professional person should be sought.

Cover photo by © Régis Cavignaux/BIOS/Peter Arnold, Inc.

Excerpt of *Blooming of a Lotus* by Thich Nhat Hanh, Copyright ©1993 by Thich Nhat Hanh.
Reprinted by permission of Beacon Press, Boston.

Excerpt from "Little Gidding" in *Four Quartets*, Copyright ©1942 by T. S. Eliot and renewed
1970 by Esme Valerie Eliot. Reprinted by permission of Harcourt, Inc.

*This book is available at quantity discounts for bulk purchases.
For information, call 1-800-872-5627.*

Contents

Part Four
Finding Balance / 165

Part Five
Connecting to the World / 211

Acknowledgments

Enormous appreciation to Seth Castleman, a dear friend, who has helped me in so many ways. Thanks to Andrew Getz, Noah Levine, Alice Higham, Keith Kachtick, and Jason Murphy for teaching with me and helping to develop this work and this book. To Jon Kabat-Zinn, James Baraz, and Joan Halifax for continued encouragement and guidance. To Carol Roth, my agent, and Cheryl Kimball, my editor, for their belief in this book. For feedback on the manuscript, many thanks to Melia Tichenor, Martina Miles, Adam Baraz, and Matt McNeil. Gratitude to Ram Dass, Stephan and Ondrea Levine, and Jack Kornfield whose audio tapes I came in touch with as a teen, and from whom I originally heard many of the teaching stories in this book. Many blessings to my partner, Maile Pickett, for . . . everything. Lastly, special thanks to the teens I work with at various centers, particularly in New York City Juvenile Halls, whose feedback continues to guide this work.

Preface

As a teen, I felt a deep longing for adventure—an adventure that lead not so much to the memorization of facts and theories, but to a wisdom based on direct experience. Following this search in my late teens and twenties led me to a variety of endeavors, including joining a world environmental walk, living in a spiritual community, hitchhiking and traveling, and to practices like meditation. This book includes stories and meditations that I've come across in the last fourteen to fifteen years while following this calling for adventure and wisdom.

I offer this book to the teens of today. May it serve as a source of valuable reflection for you.

Part One

The Vision

Introduction

The teen years are unlike any other. Life changes so fast. At times it feels like we are on an out-of-control roller coaster, and from one moment to the next, we are not sure if we are going to be jarred to the right, jarred to the left, or turned completely upside down. While we are in the midst of this great whirlwind, people have the nerve to ask us questions like, "So, what are you going to do with the rest of your life?" Like we should know, or like there's a one-word answer to describe what our life will be, or like those who ask these questions live such fascinating lives. There is tremendous pressure to get life "right," to not make any kind of mistake that will "mess it up."

Though it has been about twelve years since I was a teenager, I clearly remember the pressure I felt during that time. There seemed to be so many ways to screw up, so few ways to succeed. Life felt like a test where there were 100 possible answers and only one was correct. Yet amidst this, I thought that there must be mystery and adventure in life. It couldn't all be fear, pain, anger, and sadness . . . could it? There must be more to life than people were letting on.

Much of the material I was introduced to at the time did not address this concern. My deeper concerns about life seemed discredited by the larger society because I was young or "going through a phase," as if once you are older, you stop changing and learning so, therefore, your views are more important. I sensed there was a wisdom that was accessible in life, but that was rarely discussed. I wondered how to see and develop this wisdom. It was not like I wanted to become some great saint. The writer Henry David Thoreau said that most people live a life of quiet desperation. I knew I didn't want *that*. I wondered, *How can I make my way in life motivated not by a fear of making mistakes, but by a passion for what is real and worthwhile? How do I approach life as an adventure to be explored rather than a test to pass or fail?*

Some years later, while in my early twenties, I saw the difference between relating to life as an adventure versus a test when I had an idea to do a book of interviews with various authors, psychologists, and environmentalists whose lives I respected. I wanted to travel around and interview people who had served as inspirations and mentors to me. But I had never done anything like that before. I did not have a college degree, I had never interviewed anyone, and I had never been much of a writer. Voices of doubt overwhelmed me. "You can't do that. What if you tell people about your idea and never finish it? Who are you to do this? What will other people think?" Maybe you have felt similar blocks at times in your life. These thoughts froze me. I felt like I was coated with a thick layer of ice. Though I felt the calling to do the book, I was unable to make any progress on the idea. Luckily, a friend helped me work through my resistance and fear. He said, "You know, there is really no such thing as failure." By this, he meant that as long as I tried, I would learn something, and if I learned something, then I could never fail. Success or failure was not about publishing the book or even completing it; it was more about following my instincts and doing it for the sake of learning. This was exactly what I needed to hear at the time. I was looking at the book as a test, not as a journey. A journey is not about passing or failing; it is about learning. After I realized this, my energy was freed up to take on the project.

This book is about living life as a journey rather than as a test. It includes stories and meditations as tools in this task. These are stories and meditations that I have found and practiced over the years. I came to these stories and meditations like most people do: through difficulty and pain, and wondering if there was not some way to live happily (or at least not as lonely and depressed) in the world.

I was introduced to much of the material in this book during a difficult time in my late teens. My early teen years were, for the most part, fairly easy. My family was happy, I had many friends, and I was a popular athlete. I did well in most activities and was confident that I could meet whatever challenges came my way. But as I went from junior high to high school, my world was shattered by the unexpected divorce of my parents. I was greatly disappointed by this. Check that, I was pissed off and hurt and ashamed, and I wanted to get back at someone, anyone, for how I felt. The confidence I once felt had disappeared, practically overnight. I did not know what to do with the feelings of shame, anger, and fear that I experienced with an intensity I never previously though possible. While the pain in my heart increased, my interest in friends and sports dramatically decreased.

The world I had previously inhabited seemed like a dream. I wondered what was real. The confidence, the popularity, the success at sports, was that all an illusion? It didn't seem to matter anymore. I thought, *Why try to get all that back if it can be taken away so easily?* But what else could I do? I did not necessarily want that old world back but I did not know how else to live.

The pain in my heart continued and I was unsure what to do about it. I switched high schools twice hoping that would help. It didn't. Every day I asked my father if we could move to another city. That strategy also failed. During this time I also made many vows, one of which was to never love anyone ever again. A strategy that (I was shocked to discover) also failed. Nothing addressed the pain I felt.

For several years I was pretty much a loner. I never dated once in high school nor did I attend my junior or senior prom. I basically wanted to be left alone. During this time, I lived with my father and he tried to reach out to me the best he could. He often left books that he thought I should read outside my door. I would trip over them as I left my room. They were almost always on one of two subjects: sex or spirituality—probably the two subjects most difficult for parents and children to talk about. The sex books were mainly anatomy books describing what does what. Initially, I was more interested in them. They had pictures.

After becoming quite confident about how various sexual organs interact (thanks, Dad) and spending many nights bored in my room, I decided to give the other books a try. Reading them, I found that I had a great interest in various spiritual traditions, and I was especially intrigued by Buddhist meditation. In this material I found information that validated my experience, and spoke to the pain in my heart. The word "suffering" came to make sense to me. It was not just about a lack of food or getting sick, but was about something bigger: the underlying unease and pain in life that I felt in my heart. I found help in books and tapes that talked about the pain and suffering we go through in life, and how to turn suffering into compassion, a word that I had rarely heard but that sounded like something good to have.

I did not completely understand all the material I was introduced to and my initial attempts at meditation were difficult, but something in me felt that I was on the right track. Where this track would lead I was not sure, but I knew that I did not have to pretend or manipulate myself to follow it. I could bring all of myself to something that seemed worthwhile. My family and friends were, for the most part, kept in the dark about this interest because it was just developing, and I was unsure what they would think. I often meditated in the back bathroom, since there was a lock on the door and my family would simply think that I was taking my time going to the bathroom.

Meditation provided me a way to quiet my mind and to check in with myself to find what was true for me, rather than what people were telling me to believe. It's a practice I've continued fairly regularly over the fifteen years since that time. At times I have hated it, at times I have loved it, but I have continued to do it with (I think, anyway) some success. It is not like I've "mastered" the material in this book, a fact that any of my friends or family members can verify. However, I've been working with this material for many years and feel ready to share some of these practices and teachings.

For the last four years, I have offered meditation classes for teens in a variety of settings—from community classes at hospitals, to classes at juvenile halls and youth prison camps, where I now do most of my teaching. These classes have helped me see the tremendous struggle many teens face. There are girls in these classes who have been disowned by both parents and struggle with a drug addiction, getting high the only way they know to find a moment of relaxation in the midst of great chaos. There are guys in for murder, a requirement to gain entrance into a gang, seemingly the only community available. The struggles with violence, eating disorders, peer pressure, and drugs are enormous. Though we are living through a time of relative economic prosperity and technological advances, it seems the pressure of growing up has only increased, and there are often few resources to help one navigate through this time.

This book offers support in exploring your life, in seeing and developing your own inherent wisdom. You may read it as someone interested in meditation or you may just read it for the stories and teachings, and skip the meditations. You may also find one or two meditations that you like, and you can simply do those. It also does not need to be read from beginning to end. Please use it as you wish, and, most importantly, hold everything up to your own experience. Don't passively believe anything I say, please. I may actually write something with which I later disagree. It's happened before. So find out what is true for you. If something is useful and relates to your experience, use it; if not, then let it go.

We live in a fascinating world, full of all kinds of cool toys and gadgets, such as cell phones, pagers, computers, video games, computerized organizers, and the Web. So much is at our disposal. Yet even with all these gadgets, something else lurks in our minds and hearts that is not so easy to put into words. Some people refer to this as a "calling to mystery" or a "longing for adventure" or a "desire to know oneself." Whatever we call it, it asks that we view life not as test that we get either right or wrong, but as an adventure to be explored and discovered. Here's to that adventure. . . .

Waking Up

It is a challenge to live so that the pain and difficulty in life does not deaden us, does not cause our heart to close and our sense of aliveness to fade away. In this great challenge, we are asked to meet life with a certain attention or awareness that can help guide us through the terrain. This awareness serves as a headlight for us, like the guiding headlight of a person walking through a dark tunnel. This light of awareness helps us navigate the path of our life.

Was there ever a time when you felt suddenly alive? It was like the doors of the world opened for a minute and you could see directly into life. You were able to touch life directly and were not lost in your fears and worries. This experience may not have been during a big event like performing in a play or playing in a championship game; it may have been while walking in the woods or talking to a friend. All of sudden you felt alive, awake. This quality of waking up, or penetrating into life, we could call *mindfulness*. Mindfulness simply means being aware, being present. When you are breathing and know that you are breathing, that is mindfulness of breathing. When you are walking and know that you are walking, that is mindfulness of walking. This quality costs nothing, but it is one of the most valuable tools in the world.

Though the word mindfulness is often used in Buddhist circles, it can be found in many other traditions. People speak of waking up to God's presence or seeing the divine nature of everything. This practice of waking up can be practiced through a particular tradition or not. Some people practice mindfulness simply as a means of relaxing. Others, like the Chicago Bulls basketball team, have practiced mindfulness to help them focus on and improve their play. Some singers and musicians use mindfulness to help them calm their body and focus their mind before a performance. There are many ways to approach it.

We are living in a very interesting time. In times past, you were raised within a particular tradition and that is what, for the most part, you stayed with. Now, however, you can purchase a book on almost any spiritual tradition imaginable with the click of your mouse and a credit card number at numerous Web sites. Spiritual traditions are becoming more difficult to define and people are blending them more than ever. There are Christians who practice Buddhist meditation, Buddhists who take part in Native American sweat lodges, and others who practice a bit of everything. Some people practice Buddhist meditation or Christian prayer but do not call themselves a Buddhist or a Christian. They do not want to define themselves with a label. Others feel that identifying themselves as a Christian or Buddhist or Muslim is important to acknowledge and believe this allows them to feel more connected to that tradition. Ethnicities too can be varied. Some people say, "My mom is part Mexican and part English and my dad is part African, part European, and has some Native American blood. I currently practice African dance, Buddhist meditation, and go to Native American prayer circles, so what does that make me?" More and more of us seem to fit in this category. Clearly, during our age today the boundaries between traditions and beliefs may be more difficult to define, but the path of awakening and learning is still the same.

Whatever you do or do not do, I think it is important to honor traditions. We all have our blood ancestors consisting of past relatives and the culture in which they lived, and we have our spiritual ancestors from whom we receive guidance and support, but who may be from another culture and tradition. For some of us, they are one and the same, but others feel a spiritual connection with another tradition. In such a situation, we can still honor our blood ancestors and the culture in which we were raised while receiving the benefits of another spiritual tradition.

Both the Dalai Lama, a great Buddhist leader, and the late Mother Teresa, a great Christian leader, have said that rather than try to convert people, we should find ways to make Hindus better Hindus, Muslims better Muslims, Buddhists better Buddhists, and Christians better Christians. I think this is the spirit we need, a spirit of inclusion. We each must find our own way, whether that it is through a particular tradition or not. What's important is to take time to feed our spirit and to find ways to bring more aliveness, purpose, and adventure into our daily lives.

What Is Possible?

At times in life, we get plagued with doubts: "You cannot do that. You can never do anything right. Nothing is worth it. It's all stupid." Sound familiar? I know this state well. The phrases vary, but the underlying feeling is one of doubt and hopelessness. Of course, if you go into a new task with those beliefs, they will affect the outcome. Therefore, it can be helpful to keep an expanded view of what is possible. This does not mean that you need to know how something "should" look—what a meditation "should" be like or how life "should" turn out—but that your vision is open to all possibilities, and that you do not let fears and doubts hold you back.

It is easy to be limited by our views. When I spent a year on an environmental walk in my early twenties, we walked through many countries. The walk lasted for about three and a half years. It consisted of about seventy people across the United States and we had a number of buses to help carry our gear and food. After the United States, the group was usually about five or six people and we traveled carrying only a backpack that included a water bottle, one or two changes of clothes, a writing journal, a sleeping bag, and that was about it. Often we had very little idea how far we had walked or how far we still had to walk to arrive at the next town. We spent a good deal of time asking people directions. If we were in a country that spoke English, it was fairly easy to communicate, but in non-English speaking countries we usually relied on a map and lots of hand signals. A number of times I asked an English speaker how far it was to a particular town, and the person responded, "Oh, it is two hundred miles to that town. But if you are thinking of walking there, forget it. It is too far to walk." In their vision, this was an impossible task. I would explain that the walk had been going for two years and had crossed over 5,000 miles and that 200 was really no big deal. Strangely, the person would often still respond, "Well, you cannot walk to this town because it is too far." *Hello!*

Thoughts are very powerful. We are often limited by what we think is possible. *I am a girl, I can't do this or that,* or *I am a boy, I can't do this or that.* Thinking something is

What Is Possible?

15

possible is a first step in working toward that goal. Most of the great movements (and worst movements) arose from one person's or a group of people's thoughts. The Buddha said that everything arises from our thoughts, so paying attention to thoughts is very important.

I have heard of master sculptors who, before carving into a piece of marble, will spend many hours looking at the marble until they can see the image they want to carve already in the marble. Once they have the vision, they simply carve away whatever is not in that vision. They are then left with the image they wanted to create.

Youth provide cultures with an expanded vision of what is possible. Adults too often get worn out. Adults make statements like, *You cannot do anything about homelessness or pollution, they have always been around.* But our society is what we make it. There does not have to be homelessness or pollution. We simply have not given them our first priority. We have put economic prosperity, especially of the middle- and upper-class, before both. Issues of pollution and homelessness arise from decisions we make collectively as a culture, and these decisions can and do change.

Having a vision does not mean that life will go exactly as you wish—sometimes, far from it. There is still difficulty, pain, failure, and all the rest. But a vision helps keep the heart strong in difficult moments. I don't believe in using thoughts to create a particular outcome—visualizing the perfect mate, for example. But I also do not think thoughts should limit what in our heart we really want to do. If you think you are going to fail a test and continue to tell yourself that, you probably will. But if you consider that it is possible for you to do well on the test, you have a better chance. This does not mean that you can not study and expect to get an A; it just means that your thoughts have *some* effect on events.

One of my greatest mentors is a friend named Teru Imai. She was one of the women on the world environmental walk that I mentioned earlier. She was really the visionary of the walk and was on it for the entire journey. While many of us were in our twenties at the time, Teru was in her fifties. Just about everywhere she went, people told her, *You cannot walk across much of the world. Aren't you too old for this? What if someone robs or hurts you? Where will you sleep? How will you survive?* People were even saying this when she was almost finished with the walk. Teru never answered these questions directly. She simply kept focused on her vision. She just walked through one country, then the next, then the next, until she finished. She just did it. There were extremely difficult times—food poisoning, heat stroke, dangerous people, violent weather, and all kinds of cultural barriers—but there was also something stronger than any of this that was guiding her. She rarely even knew where she would sleep from one night to the next. She simply trusted her larger vision.

I do not think it is essential that we achieve our vision. It is not so important that my friend Teru actually finished the world walk. Most importantly, she gave it a try and followed her instincts. She put her full mind and heart to the task and did not let others' limited thinking hold her back. This is really the best we can do. We cannot guarantee completion of a vision; we can only do our best to listen to our intuition. Even if it does not turn out the way we wanted, at least we tried, and in the process of trying we probably learned more about ourselves and the world than we would have had we never tried.

A Realm of Possibilities

Sit down in a chair or on the floor and let yourself relax. Gently close your eyes and think of something that you have always wanted to do. It could be to travel to another country or to study at a particular school or to act in a play on Broadway. Whatever it is, let yourself see it. Now allow in your mind the possibility of this happening. Notice the thoughts that come in to tell that you are dreaming or that this is stupid. Let those thoughts be in the background and realize that this image you have in your head is a possibility. It's true that this vision may never happen. If we all imagine ourselves as the president of the United States, few of us will get that chance. The goal of this exercise is not to try to make this event happen, but to practice living with an open mind, a mind of many possibilities.

Long Live the Non-Normal

We tend to think that there is such a thing as a "normal" meditation or a "normal" person. Our ideas of normal often make us worry that we will do something wrong or "not normal." We may believe that a group of "normal" people exist somewhere who have their lives perfectly together and never have any doubts or fears. If there is such a group, I've never met them. If there were such a group and I met them, they would probably appear quite odd, and would not be people with whom I'd like to hang out.

There is a tendency in us to judge and ridicule that which is not normal. The kids who get picked on in school are usually the ones with the different accents, unique styles of dress, or different-looking bodies. For some reason, that which is different is seen as threatening, and the response from those "in the norm" is often one of defensiveness and ridicule. This especially happens to people who are helpless, like the new kid at school who does not know anyone.

We all participate in this to some degree. I certainly did and at times still find myself doing it. When we are with a certain group of people who identify themselves as "jocks," and the skinny kid walks by, jokes are made. Or if we are in a group who identifies itself as the "pretty ones" and the unkempt, shy girl walks by, again jokes are made. It tends to happen when the opposite of what we identify ourselves as appears in front of us. If we think we are smart, it is the person we view as dumb that tends to get our criticism. If we identify ourselves as "spiritual," it is all those "non-spiritual" people we criticize. Behind this attitude is "I'm so cool, and they're so *way* uncool."

When we are in a group of people who make such judgments of others, it is so hard to speak up and say something in defense of the person being judged. Inside we may not think it is right, but we wonder whether it is worth risking our friendships to say something. For anyone on the other side of the criticism, however, the jokes and ridicule are not that funny. And we all, eventually, get to be on both sides of this criticism.

So how do we learn to respect the non-normal? Some of the greatest scientists and saints (maybe all) were not normal. They did not fit the images of what a man or woman should be. But somehow they found a way to express their genius. Though the tendency is to try to push away the non-normal, both in ourselves and others, the non-normal is often much more interesting. In ourselves, what is not normal often comes up against our identities. *I'm a jock and I like classical music*. It makes sense to us inwardly, but the outward norms (jocks shouldn't like classical music) at times are too strong, so our interest in classical music stays hidden.

So let us stand up for the non-normal. There are already too many normal people in the world.

Stepping Outside the Box

Without even knowing it, we tend to live in little boxes. Try stepping out of that box by doing something that you have wanted to do but is a little different from your normal routine—go bowling, join a ballet class, take singing lessons, spend time with an older person. There is adventure around us if we are open to it. Do something that helps you access that sense of adventure. The possibilities are limitless.

An Unshakable Shadow

One day I was standing in line at a Mexican restaurant waiting to buy a burrito. I overheard the conversation between two young women behind me.

"Nicole, do you want anything to eat?" one girl asked.

"No," Nicole responded, "I can't afford it."

"So let me buy you dinner tonight," insisted her friend. "Really, I know you can't afford it, but I can. I have some extra cash, what's the big deal?"

The girl, however, refused the offer, while her friend kept trying to persuade her. Though I rarely get involved in the conversations of strangers, something made me turn around and say, "You know, I would like to pitch in, too.

What if I buy you something to drink and your friend buys you something to eat?"

The girl, a little shocked, was like, "Uh, okay." She accepted the offer and was very grateful for the help. I bought her drink, my burrito, and thought I'd never see either of them again.

A few days later, my mom was visiting and I wanted to take her to see some beautiful redwood trees in a state park just north of town. We decided to stop there on our way to the airport for her flight home. However, we left late and could only stop for five minutes. I was low on money at the time and noticed as I drove into the park that there was a $5 entrance fee. I thought we might be able to ask the person at the entrance if we could go in for free since we were just going to be there for five or ten minutes. I drove up to the kiosk, rolled down my window and who was on the other side? Nicole! She waved us through before I could even ask. It was an instant return of a favor.

Now, every little act of giving does not come back to us so quickly, and I could tell you many other stories of times that I stole, lied, and cheated and received the painful results of those actions. But actions seem to have a way of coming around. If you are continually mean to someone in school, there will likely be a day in the future when you will need that person's help and because of your earlier actions, you may not get it.

I do not know how it all works. I just notice that this momentum occurs. In certain Asian countries, they believe that if you kill someone, that person will come back as your child in the next life to make you learn to love that which you once hated. I have no idea if this is true, but it does seem that actions have consequences. The Buddha gives us this advice: "Speak or act with an impure mind and trouble will follow you, as the wheel follows the ox that draws the cart. . . . Speak or act with a pure mind and happiness will follow you, as your shadow, unshakable."

It's Good to Be a Beginner

When I was a teen, I read many books on Buddhist practice. In my later teens and early twenties, I came to like the idea of being a "Buddhist" and a "meditator," but what I knew about it was primarily in my head, not my heart. I liked telling people that I was a Buddhist and a meditator, but I had little actual experience. During that time, a popular book was written by the Zen master Suzuki Roshi titled *Zen Mind, Beginner's Mind*. Many people quoted the book and recommended it, but I refused to read it. I thought that since I had previously read several books on Buddhism, I certainly did not need to read a "beginner's" book on meditation. It was not until some years later that I learned that the beginner's mind was actually a sign of *progress* in the practice. It meant that one was not caught up in models and ideas about the world, and experienced life freshly, like a beginner. I then realized that I still had a great deal to learn.

At the time, I wanted to "know about" Buddhism and meditation, and did not see that at the heart of practice is not a rigid set of beliefs or knowledge, but an open, inquiring mind. As Suzuki Roshi said, "In the beginner's mind, there are many possibilities, but in the experts there are few." I had thought since I had read a few books, I "knew" about Buddhist practice. I then realized that all my ideas of "knowing" had blocked the truth more than they had revealed it.

I was like the college professor who went to see a Zen master to study Zen. When the professor met her, he told the Zen master everything he knew about Zen—all the scriptures he had read, all the knowledge he had. The Zen master responded by asking the professor if he would like tea. As the Zen master poured the tea, she overfilled the cup and continued to pour, making the tea overflow onto the table. The professor, watching the tea pour over, responded, "Stop! The cup is full. There is no room for more. Why do you keep pouring?" To which the master responded, "Like this cup, your mind is full. How can I teach you about Zen unless you first empty your cup, empty your mind?" The Zen master was telling the professor to let go of all his knowing to be open to what the master had to teach.

In beginning a meditation practice, or really anything new, it is helpful to enter with a beginner's mind. The more open and fresh our mind is, the easier it is to learn. And there is always something more to learn. With a beginner's mind, we see that teachings are always available if we are paying attention. Without an openness of mind, we close ourselves off to life and fail to see possibilities. We walk around with blinders on. If we think we "know it all" we have no room to learn all that life has to teach. Have you ever met someone who thinks they "know it all" about a subject? You bring up a subject and they immediately tell you everything they know about it, never giving you a chance to get a word in. This tendency is in all of us. We utter everything we know about something even when it is not appropriate. If you have ever been in a room full of people who are all attached to "knowing," you know how uncomfortable it can be.

Such a beginner's mind does not make us ignorant, but rather deepens our ability to see. It is not about forgetting what we know or playing stupid, but seeing that knowledge is not the only ingredient to a rich life. There is a freshness of mind that can help allow our knowledge and our wisdom to grow. It is not that we need to get rid of our knowledge, but we must not let our own views and preconceptions entrap us. In Zen they say that before practicing, mountains are mountains and rivers are rivers, then after practicing for some time, mountains are no longer mountains and rivers are no longer rivers, then after deep insight and understanding, mountains are again mountains and rivers are once again rivers. This insight is similar to a line by T. S. Eliot where he writes:

> We shall not cease from exploration
> And the end of our exploration
> Will be to arrive where we started
> And know that place as if for the first time.

How do we return to the place we started from and know that place as if for the first time? That's a great line. Both the above thoughts speak of a new type of seeing, that rather than seeing something new, the process is more about seeing with new eyes what has always been there. Can we see with a freshness that gives life to what we see? There is a level of mind that can meet each moment with great wisdom, understanding, and freshness.

Too often we see each other with old eyes, looking at our friends and loved ones but not really seeing them. We talk to them but never make real contact. Our words are not given much attention or consideration, and our awareness never engages the other person. To see someone with a beginner's mind or with fresh eyes is to see them with a willingness to learn something new.

Seeing with a Beginner's Mind

Next time you see a very good friend, really look at her. See her with a beginner's mind or with fresh eyes. Don't tell her, "I'm looking at you with a beginner's mind." She'll think you're a dork. Just do it, without advertisement or fanfare. Really see her. See the color of her eyes, the curves of her face, as if she is a miraculous person who continues to change. Notice details about her that you have maybe never seen. Realize that she, like you, is someone who is full of mystery and who changes a little each and every day.

Pssst. Hey Kid, Want a Potential?

How many times has someone told you, "You are not living up to your potential"? The person might truly care about you, but you at times interpret it as, "I don't accept you as you are. You need to be different." You take it as a judgment, and feel that if they don't accept you as you are now, perhaps they never will. A friend tells the story of being concerned about her son at a particularly difficult time in his youth. She said to him, "I'm concerned about you. You could be so much more. You have so much potential." To which he responded in disapproval, "Potential? I don't want a potential!" I love that line. Haven't we all felt this at times? We feel that the idea of potential weighs us down more than frees us up. But what kind of potential do we want?

Sometimes we think, "I am a nobody now, but once I graduate . . . or once I get that new car . . . or once I get away from my parents . . . or once I start that new Web site . . ." But the strange thing is all these *onces* continue. There is always something more to be, and there is always someone doing and accomplishing more than we are. The trap of potential says we are worthless now, but if we graduate from college, get a good job, create a million-dollar Web site, find a cure for cancer, marry a beautiful person and settle down, then and only then will we be worthy, then and only then will people accept us. Please.

Another person tells the story of a conversation with his mom when he told her he was about to go on a six-week meditation retreat, a very big commitment, and something he had worked toward for many years. Her response, however, was "Oh Jim, when are you going to get your life together?" She was concerned about him, but her ideas of what should make him happy were so very different from what actually made him happy. For him, this was a move toward greater wisdom and happiness, but she had a hard time understanding this since it was so different from her ideas. Parents and friends often greatly care about us, but they confuse their ideas of happiness with ours. I find myself doing the same thing, and realize that, while I care very much for my friends, my ideas of what might bring them happiness may or may not be what works for them, and that it is the care for their happiness that is important to share and not so much what forms they find to discover it. For example, I may think that a friend should date a particular guy or girl, but even when a friend follows what I think is right, it does not always work out. I have learned that it is good to offer my opinion, but that a friend needs to do what he or she thinks is best, and not just do it because I or someone else thinks that it's a good idea.

Of course, if a friend is doing something harmful, we want to help him or her. The art is learning how to help someone change his or her particular actions without conveying a sense of worthlessness, that he or she is flawed or bad. We all know what it is like to have that sense of failure, and the weight of "potential" hanging over us to meet the ideals of those around us. There is a balance between supporting lifestyle changes along with encouraging a sense of self-trust. Who wants to hear, "Boy, you could have really become somebody, you know." Spiritual teachings say that no matter who you are or what mistakes you have made in the past, you can be happy and live a rich life.

For several years, I struggled to complete my first book, and I lived with numerous friends and family for about two years. I had very little money, and I was writing to dozens of publishers about my book and kept getting less than enthusiastic responses. At one point, while leaving my father's house after living there for several months, my father said that he was proud of me. I had never expected him to say that, especially not when I was broke, without a home, and struggling. It did not mean that he didn't want me to improve, but that I was a worthy person even in the midst of my struggles.

Many of us will never hear this from our parents or loved ones, but it is most important that we believe it for ourselves. Even if friends or loved ones tell us we are worthy, if we do not believe it within ourselves, we dismiss it. We think, "Yeah, but if they really knew me they would not think that. If they saw the real me, they would think otherwise." Outside support can be helpful, but it is our inner belief in ourselves that seems to matter most.

The potential that we develop in a practice like meditation is more about developing inner qualities than in meeting some outer image of how we should look. The questions become: *How do I begin to believe in my goodness (or whatever name you wish to call it)? How do I begin to trust myself?* These questions cannot be answered, only lived.

Draw a Longer Line

A Zen teacher once walked up to a chalkboard and drew a straight line. He then sat down and asked all of the students to tell him the best way to make the line shorter. One student said to erase some of the line at the top, another said to erase some at the bottom, a third suggested he erase part of the line in the middle. The master shook his head after each response. The students sat in their seats confused for several minutes. Thinking that they had used up all their options, one student said, " We give up. We see no other possibilities." Then walking back up to the chalkboard, the master took his chalk and drew an even longer line next to the first one. "This is how you make the first line shorter," he said.

The story says something about how we tend to relate to people. For example, whenever you have a conflict with someone, what is the easiest thing to do? The easiest thing for most of us is to find faults with the other person—the person is rude, has no patience, is untrustworthy, and the list goes on. It is easy to encourage these thoughts, thinking this person is the only one with any responsibility for the conflict. If we continue these thoughts, we finally come to the conclusion that this person is without a doubt, in no uncertain terms (and anyone with a half a brain would agree) a total and complete L-O-S-E-R. Another approach, which for me is much more challenging, is to notice what I do not like about a person, but rather than focus on what I think is wrong with them, focus instead on building upon my strengths. Of course, the negative thoughts about a person will still arise and we may wish to no longer trust or even speak to the person, but at some point we have the choice of continuing to encourage these thoughts or to focus on what we can do to improve ourselves.

If we are playing a sport like ping pong, and we know that our opponent is weak on her backhand shot, we could continually win by hitting the ball to her backhand, but that would not necessarily improve our game. Another choice is to work on improving our overall game by playing various shots so that when we play someone who has a strong backhand shot, we can do well. As the Taoist philosopher Lao-tzu said, "The best athlete wants his opponent at his best." To be our best, rather than just thinking about how to win one match or one argument by focusing on another's weaknesses, we focus on the larger goal of learning and developing.

In the same way, if we develop positive qualities in ourselves, we have a much better chance of using each situation as a source of learning than if we continually find fault in others. This does not mean that we should use this as a way of competing, thinking that we are so great and wonderful and this other person has so many faults. It is instead a way of using situations to help us grow and mature.

Taking on a practice meditation, or any other endeavor, we may get overwhelmed by all the fear, doubt, and self-blame we notice in our mind. It is easy to see all of our difficulties or so-called "faults." We might begin to think, "Am I just a bundle of fear, anger, insecurity, and doubt?" Yeeks! But there is so much more than this inside each of us. The qualities of courage, understanding, and equanimity are present in us as well, even though they may not be as noticeable. In order to develop and bring forth these qualities, we must make room to see and acknowledge them.

Finding faults in ourselves and others is easy. The greater challenge is to draw a longer line.

Focus on Your Strengths

Take some time by yourself when it is quiet and reflect on your strong qualities. What are your strengths—perseverance? friendliness? compassion? being a good listener? understanding? You may be a little shy to actually name these, but please give it a try. This does not mean that you are without flaws. It is simply a means of seeing the positive qualities that you already possess. Make a list of these strengths.

Balancing Effort and Patience

There is a story about a young man in Japan who wanted to be the greatest martial artist in all the land. He thought that to reach this goal, he must study with the best instructor, who lived many miles away. One day he left home to go study with this great teacher. After traveling for several days, he arrived at the school and was given an audience with the teacher.

"What do you wish to learn from me?" the master asked.

"I want you to teach me your art and help me become one of the best martial artists in the country," the young man replied. "How long must I study?"

"Ten years at least," the master answered.

The guy thought, *Ten years is a lot of time. I want to get this done sooner than that. I don't have that much time.*

Certainly if I try harder I can complete this task quicker. So he asked the master, "What if I studied twice as hard as everyone else? How long would it take then?"

"Then it would take twenty years," replied the master.

The guy thought, *That's even longer! I don't want to spend twenty years learning something. I've got other things to do with my life. Certainly if I tried really hard I could learn it much quicker.* So the student asked again, "What if I practiced day and night with all my effort, then how long would it take?"

"Thirty years," was the master's response.

The young student became confused and wondered why the master kept telling him it would take longer. He asked the master, "How is it that each time I say I will try harder, you tell me that it will take longer?"

"The answer is simple. With one eye focused on your destination, there is only one eye left with which to find the way," the master said. Another way of saying this is, "With half your attention on your goal, you only have the other half to focus on the work."

Any endeavor takes effort, but it also takes patience. If we have one without the other, we get off balance. With only effort, we try and try but get frustrated when we do not see results as fast as we would like. Or we get burned out and tired very quickly. With only patience and no effort, we never really put our full attention to a task. We never give it the commitment we need. This is as true with school work as it is with a meditation practice as it is with sports. In the story, the master knew that the student had enough effort; what he needed was to balance that effort with patience.

I often noticed this when I worked one winter at a ski resort. I worked on the beginner's lift and new skiers and snowboarders came everyday. I actually did not know how to ski when I started working there, so I was interested in watching people so that I too could learn. Every day I saw new people learning to ski. Most people tried too hard. Those that put forth effort but were also relaxed and having a good time seemed to learn much faster. Inevitably, people would ask me for advice, thinking I knew how to ski. I would make general comments like, "Just relax. Don't fight the mountain. Let the mountain do the work." They would say, "Wow. Cool." But it was true. Those who relaxed and balanced effort and patience did better. Once I finally put on skis myself, I also found this to be true.

The balancing of effort and patience is a continual process. It's not like we get it right and then go on cruise control. At least I have not been able to do that. The process asks that we continually come back to balance, similar to riding a bike. It's not that we never get slightly off balance, but we learn to come back into balance sooner and more easily.

The Perfect Mate

Both in the journey of life and in the journey of meditation, we often seek perfection. We try for the "perfect" meditation or to play the "perfect" game of tennis or to find the right clothes so that we look "perfect." But this idea of perfect often creates confusion. It makes us afraid to make mistakes for fear of losing this "perfection." When we strive for the "perfect," anything less than perfect, which is whole lot of stuff, is judged, discredited, and thought of negatively.

This idea of perfection often influences our views of what a boyfriend or girlfriend should be. I was standing in line at a store the other day and I overheard the girl in front of me say to her friend, "I'm a teenager. All I *do* is think of boys." Not all teenagers think of the opposite sex all the time, but this is the time when we begin to give serious thought to what kind of partner we want, or whether we even want a partner. Sometimes, we think there is a perfect man or woman out there who, when we meet, will make everything perfect.

There is a story about an old man named Jacob who had never married. One day his friend came by for a visit and asked, "Jacob, I've always wondered, why did you never get married? You seem like a good man. Didn't you ever try to find a wife?"

Jacob looked off into the distance as if trying to remember a time long ago. "Actually, when I was young I was determined to find the perfect mate. I wanted her to be smart, funny, nice, good-looking, a good cook, like the same music as I did, and many other things. I had a list a page long. I first looked for her in San Francisco where I met a really nice woman."

"What happened? Did you marry her?"

"No, she was almost perfect, but she was not very smart and I wanted to be with someone smart. So then I went to New York where again I met a wonderful woman. She was smart, but it turned out that she was just a little rude for my tastes. I wanted a nice woman."

"What did you do then?"

"Then I went to Paris because it was supposed to be the city of love. Again I met someone. She was nice, but she was not as attractive as I wanted." Jacob's eyes widened as he looked his friend in the eye. "But then I went to London, and, believe it or not, in London I found her. She was smart, attractive, nice, liked the same music. She was everything on my list of a perfect woman. I couldn't believe it."

"What happened? If she was perfect, why didn't you marry her?"

"Alas. There was one small problem. She happened to be looking for the perfect man."

This is really the heartbreaker—thinking we have found the perfect person but then they do not want us. What does it mean to find the perfect person? Sometimes we meet someone who is the perfect person in our mind in terms of what we think we like (he or she is tall, popular, smart), but on a deeper level, it is not right at all. When we are around them we do not feel supported or honored. It looks good to our friends to be with them, but it does not feel good to us. We look good in pictures together, but as soon as we begin to speak to one another, it goes. The author and psychologist Clarissa Pinkola Estes suggests that we pick a partner as if we were blind, to go by our instincts and intuition more than the images in our head. Sometimes what feels right inwardly is not what we had expected.

One of my teachers has said that we need not try to become perfect ourselves or find someone we think is perfect, but instead to find that within ourselves that is perfection, that is already perfect. What, in ourselves, is worthy and good? How do we begin to live so when we do meet a person we want to spend time with, they will see the real us? There is nothing worse than a relationship where partners have a false idea of one another and are constantly trying to live up to distorted images of beauty or intelligence or some other quality. It's like both people are in a movie playing different roles rather than being themselves. If we can find the real, the genuine, within ourselves maybe we will be able to see it in others. Then, hopefully, whatever decisions we make from this place will be the right ones for us.

Part Two

Mindfulness in Life

True Listening

For many of us the word "listen" does not have a good reputation. How many times have you been told by parents and teachers, "Listen to me!" They often really mean, "Do what I say!" But no one can really make you listen. Your body may be in the room, your eyes may even be looking at the person, but your mind can be anywhere in the world. You can tune them out if you really want to. Tuning someone out can be a way of protecting ourselves in certain situations. It is a skill that, at certain moments, can be useful.

However, at other times real listening is the most important action you can do. There are so many wars and conflicts in the world (and in our own lives) where both sides refuse to listen to each other. They refuse to give the other side a chance to explain their views. If one group really tried to listen and understand the other, the conflict could be minimized or possibly solved.

It hurts to be ignored. Ever had someone ask you how you are, and as you begin to tell them, they pick up a magazine or turn on the television? They don't even listen to you. You're like, "Excuse me. I'm t-a-l-k-i-n-g." You feel disrespected. If they cared about you, you think, they would at least listen to you.

Giving someone your full attention is a sign of respect. You respect them enough to listen to them, to do your best to understand what they have to say, whether it is good news or bad news. This attention is possibly the most valuable quality in the world. Companies pay thousands of dollars for a thirty-second TV commercial. And this buys what? They hope it buys thirty seconds' worth of your attention. Commercials are now displayed in planes, grocery stores, and video stores, all hoping to get a few seconds of this valuable attention. One could argue that the Internet continues because of those few seconds we give our attention to the ad on the page, usually at the top of the screen. This pays people's salaries and keeps businesses investing. So attention is the most valuable quality in the world. When you are speaking with someone you have the opportunity to give them this most valuable quality.

True listening is not very easy. Much of the time, when someone is talking to us, we are rehearsing what we are going to say in response, judging the person's comments, or we cut them off before they are even finished. One way to practice listening is to wait until someone is finished speaking before we reply. Sound easy? Believe me, it's not. Better yet, don't believe me—try it for yourself.

There are listening exercises in which one person speaks and the other listens. The listener cannot respond until the person speaking has said she is finished. Once that happens, the listener then summarizes what she heard the speaker say. This can actually be quite funny. If someone is not paying attention, the listener may say something very different from what was actually said. Sometimes our own views get in the way. The speaker might say, "I was sad that my boyfriend could not come to the party with me." The listener may respond, "You said that you were angry at your boyfriend and wanted to get back at him." That may be how the listener would feel if she was in that situation, but it is not what the speaker said. Understanding the difference between what someone actually says and what we *think about* what that person says is not easy. Noticing this can help determine whether the conversation results in understanding or in conflict.

This is not to say that listening has to become a big chore or that we need to take it so seriously that it becomes phony. But at times our full attention can be the greatest action we can do for someone. True listening should not be something we feel pressured to do. It should be something we do out of respect, a respect that we, too, want and deserve.

Try This

Listening Practice

For one day, practice listening. For this day, your goal is to listen deeply to people, to give them your full attention. See if you can hear not just their words, but the spirit or feeling behind their words. Really try to understand them, to see the world from their eyes. Some people call this "listening from the heart." This does not have to become a strenuous task. It just means that we give people the same respect that we want too. For one day, practice listening.

Minds Like Parachutes

There is saying that goes, "Minds are like parachutes. They only work when open." This sounds neat, but what does it mean to have an open mind?

Keeping an open mind is not at all easy, but it is extremely important. Say you were invited to attend a party, and you had many ideas of what this party would be like. You thought there was going to be a live band, many of your friends, and people who shared your interests. Maybe someone told you this information or maybe you just had this idea from past experiences of similar parties. But when you show up at the party you see no band, very few of your friends, and people you usually do not associate with. They are all jocks and you are a punk, or they are all punks and you are a jock—whatever. One choice is to leave the party immediately and wonder why you ever came. I would do this a lot, and sometimes still find myself doing it. *This does not fit the image I had in my head, so I'm out of here.* A more open-minded choice, which at times is more difficult, is to say, "It's not what I thought, but maybe I can still have a good time." We can use it as an opportunity to get to know people whom we would otherwise never talk to. An open mind asks us to at least consider such experiences as a learning opportunity.

Or say you were always told when you were growing up that a certain type of people were uncaring, untrustworthy, and mean. It could be any group—a particular economic class, social class, religion, ethnicity, sexual orientation, or people from a particular geographic area. Then one day you meet someone from this group who does not fit this image at all. As an example, let's say you were told to distrust rich people, then one day you meet a very kind and generous rich person. In this situation, do we hold on to that previously held belief or is our mind open enough to re-evaluate? It's not like we need to get rid of all our beliefs, but when the world presents us with new information, can we allow that in and make room for it or do we push it away?

Of course, we can always find examples that fit our stereotypes (we can find rich people who are in fact uncaring) but it is another thing to say that this is true of everyone in a particular group. *All of this kind of people are this way.* When we meet a rich person, do we instantly view them as untrustworthy for no action of their own? Have you ever been looked at as untrustworthy just because of your religion or style of dress or economic class? It sucks. So maybe there is a way to take into consideration our past experiences and not put ourselves in danger, but still relate to people as people and give them a chance.

This is not to say that we should continue to trust someone who has hurt us or put us in dangerous situations. If someone is uncool or mean to us, they will most likely be so again, and it would stupid of us to keep letting ourselves be hurt or taken advantage of. But whoever is uncool to us, it does not mean that those people with a similar style of dress or religion or economic class or anything else will behave the same way. This may seem kind of obvious, but rigid beliefs about particular groups of people cause enormous pain and conflicts, not just in the form of wars, but also in the form of judgments and ridicule among our friends. The stereotypes and resentments sometimes build up for years and over generations, and they are not so easy to work through. Youth, in particular, have the chance to start anew and to heal many of the barriers created by past generations. Young people have the chance to acknowledge and learn from the past, while committing to give people the opportunity to act differently. Otherwise, people continue to act as they are viewed.

Ever been around someone who only notices your mistakes? How does it make you feel? What usually happens? You usually make more mistakes. If a child is told all her life that she is worthless, for example, after many years of hearing this she will begin to believe that, you guessed it, she is worthless. On the other hand, have you ever been around someone who sees your positive qualities and believes in you? How does it make you feel? What usually happens? You probably want to try and live up to that positive view. It is not easy to keep an open mind and to trust in people, but what's the other option? Someone has to turn the tide of hatred and ridicule toward individuals and groups of people. It might as well be you.

Keeping an Open Mind

Next time you are in a situation where you do not know people, see if you can bring a sense of adventure and curiosity to the situation. If there are people there whom you usually do not associate with, see if you can learn something about them. What are these people like? What are their interests? You may have all these ideas about what a certain group of people is like, but take this chance to see for yourself what is true.

Maybe there is more to a particular group than you think, maybe there are people who actually have similar hopes and dreams to your own. When given the opportunity to have contact with a group of people whom you usually do not associate with, take it. Don't put yourself in danger, but relate to people from this group with an open mind.

Raising Parents

It's interesting to remember that parents were once kids. Imagine your parents young, growing up, entering puberty, going on their first date, getting together to have you. It's weird to think about it, but they too were once young. Many of them brought us into this world really wanting to raise a happy child and do a good job as parents. Most parents spent many hours changing diapers, teaching us how to walk, driving us here and there. Unfortunately, this care often gets lost over the years and it can be hard to rekindle.

Because of the enormous bond between parent and child, we have many ways to both help and hurt one another. It is like we have direct access to each other's hearts. They tell us that we are stupid—and it hurts; we tell them that they are not good parents—and they feel it. The power we have for affecting each other is immense.

The parent/child relationship is in its best moments a team; in its worst moments, it's a fierce competition. Some parents are just so out of it that no partnership or team quality is possible, but most that I know really do want to help their children; they want to be supportive. Part of the process seems to be learning how to live our own goals while respecting their views. Eventually, we will get to call the shots for our life, but the teen and young adult years are a transition period where we start to get some, but not complete, freedom of choice.

The question seems to be, how do we learn to respect and consider parents' views without thinking we need to go to war with them? As a late teen, I remember feeling like I really wanted to let my parents know that I was in control of my life. I quit college and went back several times, partly because I wanted to let them know that I was making the decisions now. But when we are simply acting in a certain way to get back at them or to prove a point, we are still not in control. By doing the opposite of what they say instead of doing what they say, we are still controlled by them. All they have to do is tell us not to do something, and we are right there doing it.

When my parents divorced I was greatly disappointed, and not knowing how to talk to them directly, I wanted to show them how I felt. *You want to see disappointment, I'll show you disappointment.* For awhile, the last thing I wanted to do was to make my parents happy or pleased with me. I did not care what happened in my life as long as it made them feel disappointed. But I was not really living my own life. I had the idea, *My life may be miserable, but I'm sure showing them.* But after awhile, the question arises, *I am continuing to screw up my life to get back at my parents, and this is benefiting whom?*

So how do we learn to make parents our allies, to receive the wisdom they have while following our own heart and vision? Most parents actually have a great deal of insight and wisdom that they really want to pass on to their children. One way to gain a better understanding of our parents is to find out about their childhood and the pressures they were under. We often know little about our parents' early life, and this can affect how they relate to us. For example, one of our parents may have grown up poor and seen firsthand how hard that is. As a parent, they may pressure us to make a lot of money because they don't want us to go through that same difficulty. But we feel this as an enormous pressure to become some workaholic businessman or businesswoman. Many people revolt against such pressure. *I'll show you that money is not important.* We may spend many years doing jobs that we really don't want to do just to prove this point. But there may be a better way to work with this—where we are not just following orders, living life for them, nor reacting to them by doing the opposite of what they say and not really living our own life. Part of the solution may be talking to each other about our fears and sorting out what we truly want to pursue in life.

No parent/child relationship is the same. And there are abusive parents in the world who do not have our best interests in mind. But somehow we find ourselves in this life, with whatever parents we have, and just as we are learning and developing, so are they. Hopefully, we can find ways to aid in this learning rather than be a hindrance to it. If we can, life will be easier for all of us.

Parent Stories

If you are lucky enough to have contact with a parent or your parents, find a time when you can be alone with them and that is comfortable for both of you. It can be helpful to take a walk or at least be in an environment that is relaxing. Ask them about their early life—what their memories are of that time, both the good and the not-so-good ones. What stories do they remember? What was it like for them when they were the age you are now? Then just listen. Try not to make any comments about how they should have done this or that or how you would have done this or that. Just give them the space to tell you whatever they are comfortable with in that moment. See if you can see them as a person similar to you, who has known joy and difficulty in life. If you do not have access to your parents, see if you can find someone who was close to them when they were young and get stories from that person.

Neither Pushing Away Nor Grasping

I remember reading Zen books when I was younger and hearing about an ultimate state of being free from desire. I began to wonder whether I should desire to be desireless. Should I desire that desire go away? What's that? How would I make decisions if it were not for desire?

I have since seen that there are different types of desire. In its pure form, desire is natural and wonderful. You would not be reading this book if it weren't for desire. It's desire that makes you care about your friends and family and have a vision for the future. However, there is desire that comes from a place of completeness and desire that comes from a place of incompleteness. Desire that comes from a place of incompleteness becomes greed and craving, and, when acted upon, can cause us difficulty.

You can tell the difference between types of desire by their pattern. There is the desire that says, "I have to have it, now!" This type of desire has a particular momentum behind it. It has an emergency quality, a feeling of incompleteness yearning for satisfaction.

With this type of desire, even fulfilling a particular act does not satisfy it. There are people with very strong desires to have a great deal of money, for example, and they work twelve to fifteen hours a day toward that goal, often at the expense of friends and family. But often, even after they acquire lots of money, the desire does not go away. They now want even more money! This type of desire is in all of us. It is like a burning ember. The objects we choose to cool its heat do not diminish it, but instead turn this ember into a full-blown fire. The more we do, the bigger the fire gets.

Often desires arise and we act on them unknowingly. While watching television, we see an advertisement for pizza. Before we know it, we are on the phone ordering a large pepperoni with extra olives. A few hours later, after eating far too many pieces, we wonder why we decided to order a large pizza in the first place. Without any awareness of desire, we have little true choice in our life. Unconsciously acting on every desire that we see on TV or that arises in our mind is not real choice. Real choice only comes through awareness. The more we are aware of desire, the more choice we have in whether or not to act on it.

As we gain a better understanding of desire, we notice the different qualities of desire. We notice the difference between addictive desire, which can never truly be satisfied, and the desire that comes from a place of completion. The latter is not a desire that attempts to fill an empty hole, but is more of a guide as to which way we should go or what to do next. When we are thirsty, we desire water. When hungry, we desire food. When our hand is on a burner, we desire to move it off. This desire is simply a means of survival and appropriateness. It addresses the situation at hand. This type of desire has a different momentum to it. It is not about trying to fill a bottomless pit, rather it is information for us to act on.

The opposite of addictive desire is addictive aversion. Aversion is a pushing away, an attempt to avoid or evade. It can take many forms—anger, resentment, revenge. Aversion can simply be not wanting to see a particular person or to remember a certain event. Our conditioned response to unpleasant experiences is to avoid them whenever possible. This is simply a survival mechanism. While this can be helpful at times, at other times growth calls for us to sit with unpleasant states. Sometimes the avoidance of an experience causes us more difficulty than the full experience of it.

Again, aversion is not something that we must plow through. Working with aversion is not a tough guy's approach. Awareness of aversion simply gives us greater choice about whether to act on it or not. We could be walking into a dark alley, and all of a sudden get the feeling that we should turn around and walk back the other away. We may have an aversion to walking down the alley, but it may be good advice to follow. Again, the more we get acquainted with various states of mind, the more we will know which ones to act on and which ones not to. The more we get to know our anger and fear, the less they will unconsciously motivate our life. Repressing certain states does not mean that they no longer affect us, only that we no longer have access to them.

This does not mean that all desire or aversion is bad, only that we can become aware of both so as to develop more choice. When we "have to have" a particular piece of clothing and suffer if we don't, that is something for us to explore. We begin to explore, "How can I be happy whether or not I get a particular object? Where is real happiness found?"

In us all is the place that knows. The more we sit and listen to that inner voice, the more we learn to trust it. There is an inner balance we can begin to trust and bring forth.

Take Yourself Lightly

There is a saying that angels can fly because they take themselves so lightly. A sense of lightness and playfulness is essential. Life can get very tight and rigid. When you find yourself taking it too seriously, it is helpful to smile and enjoy the moment. As the saying goes, "The path is the goal." We are all a part of a learning process. We are all stumbling toward the light. Sometimes it seems like we are making great strides, while other times it seems we are going nowhere. An appreciation of where we are and a sense of joy in the discovery is essential.

Laughing at oneself is a great art. Youth often think that other people, especially older people, have it all together and know what is going on all the time. This is not true.

Adults struggle just as much as youth. Everyone is doing the best they can with what they've got. We are all in this process of discovery.

Laughing at ourselves, not in a negative way, but with lightness and non-attachment can be a wonderful practice. By non-attachment I mean not attaching to how we thought life was supposed to turn out, and realizing that there is a great deal of unknown in the world, and one never really knows what life will bring. No one has it all worked out. So often when we think we are beyond a pattern, we find ourselves doing what we thought we were "beyond." Life has a way of continually showing us what we still need to learn. Life demands that we take ourselves lightly.

Some people use the practice of keeping a "half-smile" while going throughout the day to remind themselves to cultivate joy. Some refer to this as the "half-smile of the Buddha." To bring a half-smile to one's meditation or to a task like washing the dishes brings forth a sense of lightness and ease.

Any practice can become very serious business. Some days, if we do a practice like meditation and it is very noisy in the house, we may find ourselves screaming at our family or roommates, "Shut up! Can't you see that I am trying to meditate and learn compassion!" We can get uptight very quickly. While it can be important to find a quiet space, it is easy to forget the importance of playfulness.

Whenever I find myself getting too serious, I think of the comments of the novelist Kurt Vonnegut Jr. In his book *Timequake*, his character says that we are on this earth for one reason and one reason only, and to not let anyone tell you anything differently. Our purpose on this earth is this: to fart around. This is not exactly the message of the great spiritual teachers, but I think it has some truth to it. To me this does not mean laziness, but to at times let go of our worries and concerns and just enjoy ourselves.

Don't Just Do Something, Sit There

When I spent many months on an environmental walk across the United States in my early twenties, people were often dismayed at seeing our ragtag group walk through their peaceful town. They did not know what to make of our band of painted school buses (used to carry food and supplies), banners, and non-showered population. People would often approach us with curious questions. One time a friend asked junior high students if they had any questions about our walk, and one girl asked, "Yes, I just want to know if you are camping all the time, where do you plug in your hair dryers?" The girl was shocked to find out that no one carried one.

Usually the questions we got from people we met were more general, like what was our destination. When we would inform them that we were walking from California to New York or from Tokyo to Hiroshima, they would look at us in dismay. People at times responded, "Why walk? You know, you could get there much faster by car or by plane." The wise guy in me often wanted to respond, "Gee, thanks, we actually thought we *could* get there faster by walking." The point was not to get somewhere. We would tell them that we would miss out on so many moments if we drove or flew. We would probably not have met them if we were driving, we would probably not have taken in the landscape as fully, probably not seen as many sunsets. Even if we drove through and saw the land, we would not get to know the land or the people as well. We would not feel as a part of it. We did not have to pull over to the side of the road to take a picture or to watch a sunset; we were already on the side of the road! We walked in a way that helped us receive and take in the moment.

To most people this was very strange. *Life is about getting somewhere. If you want to get to New York, go the fastest way possible. Get there fast.* Fast food, fast cars, fast lives. Why is it so strange and difficult to stop? To stop before eating, to stop to smell a flower, to stop and watch the sunset? Why is it so odd to not try to get somewhere?

Of course, stopping is not just about slowing down physically, but slowing down our mind to take in the moment. Anyone who has watched Michael Jordan play basketball or seen a talented dancer or martial artist knows the grace and concentration one can have while moving quickly. It is the combination of concentration and grace that make such people a joy to watch. They are completely involved with what they are doing, making each movement count, becoming in tune with the natural flow. It is not so much about how fast the body does or does not move but the level of concentration and focus that is present.

However, sometimes it can be helpful to slow down and take in the moment. This does not mean that we need to walk around like zombies or never do fun activities, but that when we find ourselves getting overwhelmed and feel that our life is passing us by, it can be useful to stop and take a break. It can be to watch a sunset or to sit at a beach or a park. In the end, life is made up of a bunch of moments. Taking the time to enjoy these moments is a great practice. When most people come to the end of their life, they don't think, "Boy, I wish that I would have been more in a hurry and not stopped to watch so many sunsets. If only I had been more stressed out." It is usually, "I wished I would have slowed down more and enjoyed life more, appreciated what I had around me. It was over so quickly."

Wisdom Is Not Something You Get, It Is Something You Already Have

There is a difference between wisdom and knowledge. One could say that wisdom is knowledge that has been brought into one's heart and experienced as true. For wisdom, an idea or thought must be tested and investigated. We cannot gain wisdom by passively accepting what we read or by believing what another tells us. We have all been introduced to many ideas and theories from reading books or listening to someone, but until this information has been tested in our own experience, wisdom is not possible. Wisdom requires an attention to life and a willingness to ask and experience firsthand what is true.

It is easy to notice when someone tells us something from actual experience or when it is just an idea. Ideas and knowledge are wonderful, but certain truths must be tested in our heart before they have power. Someone can tell you, for example, that what is really important in life are friends. They can really believe this, but they do not really live this truth. They are not there for friends when they need to be. You call them to talk about some difficulties you are having in your life and, after one minute of listening to you, they spend thirty minutes talking about themselves. Then afterwards they say, "Friends are so important." Though they are sincere in telling you this statement, their words only go so far because their experience of this truth has not matured. Another person can tell you the same thing and their words have more depth. This person has seen the importance of friends and she works hard to help those that are close to her. It is not just an idea for her; it is something she actively lives. When people speak from this place, our whole body hears their words. It is as if there is a channel between the two of us that allows us to receive not just their words, but the depth of their experience. They have gained wisdom by investigating and testing the profundity of this truth in their life. Their knowledge has been cultivated and tested, and has matured into wisdom.

It can be helpful to ask, what is true? What does my direct experience tell me? The Buddha said that you should not believe something just because it is written in a book, or because the person who said it is well-known, or a teacher, or an elder, or anything. He said to only believe something after you have tested it in your own heart and found it to be true. Wisdom can only be attained by this type of inner experimentation and willingness to experience and see for oneself. The Buddha said, "Those who recite many scriptures but fail to practice their teachings are like a cowherd counting another's cows." Lao-tzu speaks of the different types of knowledge when he writes, "Knowing others is intelligence, knowing yourself is true wisdom."

When I first started practicing meditation I wanted to be the one who "knew." I would utter what I thought were wise phrases to my friends hoping they would come to me for advice. I thought that by thinking certain high and deep thoughts, I could gain this esteemed position. However, I noticed that the more I tried to be wise, the less I could access wisdom. My words would stumble out in the form of advice, leaving the person confused and uncertain. I was not interested in exploring the truth together or in sharing from my experience; I was more interested in impressing them. I thought wisdom meant knowing all the answers all the time. I did not know at the time that it required much more than that.

I soon saw that "trying" to be wise all the time was very unwise. I learned that wisdom did not mean "knowing" all the answers. Rather it was a state of mind, an openness of mind, that explored and investigated the truth. Wisdom did not have set answers for everything, but it had a willingness to learn. Over time, rather than trying to resist and hide my not knowing, I have learned to allow and trust it. So if I don't know how to use a particular tool or am unsure what a word someone says means, I try (though not always successfully) to say that I do not know how something works or the meaning of a word, but I'd like to learn. Previously, I always tried to avoid such situations whenever possible.

Many people think of wisdom as a type of one-upmanship. *He or she didn't know the answer, but I did. I must be smarter.* They think of it as an either/or dichotomy. Either I am right or you are right. And the person who is right more is the wisest. However, wisdom has little to do with being right—at least not the kind of right that puts someone else down. Often we try to be right not to help another person, but to show that we are better than them. We may be right about the details of what is in question—where the store is, the capital of Oregon, the last name of a friend—but the attitude or energy behind it is something else. Our words create more division than harmony. We were right about certain details, but not right in how we went about it.

Wisdom is different. It looks at not just the details, but at how something is said. It inquires as to what builds more harmony and union, and what creates more discord and conflict.

In this attitude, no one is really right. It is a team effort in the exploration of what is true. Sometimes I have wisdom to offer, and sometimes you do. It is not a static relationship with one person on one side and the other person on the other. Rather it is a dance in which we both play a part.

Wisdom is not something one person can grab and keep for themselves. Trying to capture and hold on to it makes it immediately slip away. Wisdom is a process. It asks to be both a student and a teacher. It is a community effort.

Experiment in Truth

Take some time to reflect on the question, *What is true?* What does your experience tell you? What have you learned so far in this life? What have you noticed?

The answer you will receive is not always a straight answer, like X or Y. Rather the question leads to a deeper and more profound experience of the question. The answer you get is not just known intellectually, but known in your heart and body. Keep asking the question, *What do I know is true?* and see where it takes you. Make a list of what you find.

Enjoy Joy

Many people see spiritual practice as one of deprivation. My understanding is that while renunciation is important in any practice, a spiritual life should help us know joy, and not just be dreary and lifeless. Certainly there is pain and suffering in the world, but there is also much more. One of my favorite stories of the Buddha is one where he comes on stage in front of a large audience of monks, and instead of talking he holds up a flower. While many of the people in the audience wonder, "What is he doing? When is he going to speak?" one monk simply smiles. This monk, the story goes, understood the Buddha. I have always liked this story and wondered what the monk understood that others did not. I have recently begun to think that it has something to do with joy.

The poet Lu Yu writes,

The clouds above us join and separate.
The breeze in the courtyard leaves and returns.
Life is like that, so why not relax?
Who can stop us from celebrating?

The flower is in front of us, why not enjoy it just for what it is? Why not enjoy the breeze just as it is? This is my interpretation of the story from the Buddha. Maybe there are other interpretations, but Lu Yu seems to be telling us that there is beauty in the world just as it is—in a flower, in the wind, in our friends. More than trying to understand something or to get something, there is always something to enjoy. As Lu Yu puts it, "Who can stop us from celebrating?" The monk in the story was not waiting for an explanation about the flower. He just enjoyed it for what it is.

Joy is different from just satisfying a desire. There is a certain satisfaction in wanting to have pizza for dinner, then getting it, or from our favorite team winning the big game. Joy, however, is something else. Certainly we can find some joy in eating pizza or our team winning, but can we also find joy in not getting pizza or in our team losing? Can we lose the big game, and walk outside and enjoy the evening breeze or the moonlight, or do we lose our joy for the evening, for the month, or for years because of that disappointing experience? To what extent are we open to joy? For many us, pain, misery, and depression are easy to feel. Joy is at times more difficult. We resist it, thinking that there is something wrong with us if we are joyful. Strange.

In Buddhism there are four qualities that are called the Brahma-Viharas or "Heavenly-Abodes." The Brahma-Viharas are the qualities of the heart that we develop. They include lovingkindness, compassion, sympathetic joy, and equanimity. When I heard about them, I easily grasped the importance of lovingkindness. Be loving to people; I get that. The second, compassion, also made sense, as did the fourth, equanimity. But I initially wondered why sympathetic joy was listed in this group. I thought the Buddha talked about suffering, not joy. And what is *sympathetic* joy?

I have only recently begun to see the importance of this quality. Sympathetic joy is an openness to joy, not just in oneself but in others. It is to share in the joy of others almost as if it was one's own. It is a fairly wild concept; it says that if someone is experiencing joy, why hold back—join in! If someone is joyful over getting a new job or getting first place in a contest, we can share in that joy with them.

Of course, there are always those times when we think, "*I* wanted that job" or "*I* wanted to get first place." We are not so joyful, and would prefer to switch positions with the other person. This teaching seems to be asking us to put another's joy on equal footing as our own. While feelings of remorse and envy may be present, there is another level to the game. We can share in the joy of others as if it was our own. Joy is not to be experienced by the few, but by the many. The tank will not dry up as more people experience it.

Sympathetic joy is a fascinating concept that I am still coming to understand and experience, but it can be an interesting quality to explore. When I was little my mother used to point at particular people and say, "See that person. They have spirit." As a child I wondered what she meant, and I think now that she was noticing a particular joy or aliveness in people. Without this quality, without any sympathetic joy, everyone's successes somehow become our failures. The more others are happy, the worse we feel about ourselves. Life becomes a competition. Sympathetic joy asks us to end the game. It asks us to look beyond ourselves and to share in the happiness of others. By sharing in the happiness of others we, strangely enough, oftentimes find the happiness that we too seek.

Sympathetic Joy Practice

The next time someone gives you good news, share in that good news with them almost as if it was your own. It's more like being happy *with* them than being happy *for* them. Let yourself feel and experience this joy. If there are thoughts of envy on your part, notice them, and see if there is not a deeper place inside you that simply wants all people to be happy.

Practice Compassion

Compassion is the ability to feel the suffering in ourselves and others with an open heart. Often when we see someone suffering, if they are sick or sad or hurting, our first impulse is to leave the room or somehow get away. Compassion is the ability to sit with an open heart in the presence of unpleasant states. Suffering is a part of life, and no matter how hard we try to deny or run away from it, we never can. Just reading the morning news, we hear about the enormous suffering of ocean animals and plant life struggling to survive after an oil spill, someone killing a former friend they got angry with, numerous countries at war. We can also see it in our everyday lives—our friend who is struggling, our boss who is worried about the business, and in our family as parents and children try to get along.

Sometimes we think that if we can get our lives really together, we can prevent unpleasant experiences from happening to us. We think, *If I eat right and meditate only good things will happen to me.* While it does seem that certain actions help lead to a richer life, it does not mean that pain will no longer come our way. The car next to us can still have a blowout and swerve into us, leaving us permanently injured or dead. Our friends and parents will still get sick and pass away. We cannot fully prevent our child from being born with a handicap or ourselves from getting an illness that leaves us bedridden. If there was a drug that could prevent such occurrences, it would be the hottest item on the market. The stocks of the company who produced it would soar. But there is not. Though without a doubt there are actions that decrease the likelihood of certain events, the universe seems to have the final say.

So how do we live in a world of such uncertainty, where we are not given any assurances? One way is to practice meeting the little difficulties of life with a compassionate heart. Who knows why pain comes our way? It just seems to be in the blueprints. Though we cannot completely control what events come our way, we can practice meeting such moments with an open heart, with a heart that has room for the immensity of pain and joy in the world. If we start with the little difficulties, we will be better able to work with the big ones. We may not be able to have compassion for a friend who betrayed us, but we can start with the person at the store who was rude to us, the driver who cut us off on the road, or the impatient customer.

Compassion is the ability to acknowledge suffering and see that it is not the enemy. Suffering is a part of life, but our response to it can be one that eases it. Though life is painful at times, our heart is much stronger. Our heart may ache, but we need not respond by shutting out the suffering in life. Ursula K. LeGuin writes in her novel *The Dispossessed*, "If you evade suffering you also evade the chance of joy. Pleasure you may get, or pleasures, but you will not be fulfilled. You will not know what it is to come home."

In our friendships, we need to be there for our friends not just when they are happy, but when they are unhappy as well. For true friendship, we cannot leave when it gets difficult. We want our friends to help us when we are having a hard time, and they need our help as well. Compassion is the act of not turning our back on difficulty. Initially, our ability to open our heart to difficulty may seem limited, but it is something that we can develop with practice.

We can experience compassion for another or for ourselves. Compassion for ourselves involves acknowledging how hard life can be at times and how much we wish to be happy. Often it is most difficult to have compassion for ourselves. If we could all tell our life stories to each other, we would realize that each of us has suffered a great deal. Even the people who seem to have had an easy life, once we really hear their stories, reveal that they have suffered much more than we had thought.

If there is one thing that we all have in common, it is suffering. Compassion is our ability to open to suffering so that suffering does not get us down, but rather opens our heart. Though difficult at times, by gently opening to suffering we are more capable of experiencing compassion for ourselves and others. During hard times, sometimes the best we can do is send ourselves kindness and care. When times are very difficult, we need compassion the most.

Many of us think of compassion as a type of pressure or commandment, that compassion means that we never feel angry or that we must tell someone we love them when we really don't at that moment. We think, *I am angry at him. I don't want to pretend to be all kind and sweet. That's fake. No way am I going to show them compassion.*

Compassion is not about telling ourselves that we should not be angry or should not be sad, but learning how to relate to the anger and sadness in ourselves and others with understanding. Compassion means to first bring understanding to our own feelings. Of course, you cannot deny angry feelings. You may need to take some time by yourself or talk with a third party before you can speak to the person with whom you are upset. Compassion does not mean only saying "nice" comments to people or telling them what we think they want to hear. It is a matter of respecting both our own feelings and the feelings of the people around us.

We all suffer at times, the question is how do we relate to ourselves in those moments. Do we touch our or another's pain with love or with fear? Writer and meditation teacher Stephen Levine has said, "When your fear touches someone's pain, it is pity; when your love touches someone's pain, it is compassion." Often when we see someone in pain, it triggers our own fear of being in pain. When we relate to them from this place of fear, we further encourage their aversion and resistance to their experience. The more our heart meets the moment with care, the more we can both share in the acceptance and truth of whatever is happening.

Some years ago a meditation teacher told me that nothing can be pushed away or denied in this process. At the time I disagreed with him. I had a strong aversion to sexuality, and did not accept those desires in myself or others. I thought anyone who acted on such impulses was lost in confusion and lust. In reality, I feared the intimacy of getting close to another person. I had always pushed away any feelings of attractions I had, thinking such desires were not worth acknowledging. In high school, if a girl ever smiled at me or looked interested, I would send her mean looks and turn away. Over the years my teacher's words became more evident. I realized that I had created a wall around myself. I had thought I was putting this wall up to protect me (and for a certain time it did serve that purpose), but after a few years this same wall was that which imprisoned me. My lack of acceptance of my own and others feelings around sexuality had me walking through life always avoiding anything that involved intimacy. It was only by allowing and accepting my own and others' sexuality that I learned to relate to myself and others from openness rather than fear and denial.

It is in our ability to open to our own suffering that we are then able to relate to the suffering of others with compassion. The Dalai Lama writes, "One of the most important things is compassion. We cannot buy it in one of New York City's big shops. We cannot produce it by machines. But by inner development, yes. Without inner peace, it is impossible to have world peace."

Without Batting an Eye

We hear a great deal about the importance of courage. People say that we need courage to do dangerous acts, like bungee jumping or rock climbing or hitchhiking. I remember going out one night with friends, drinking way too many beers, and climbing to the top of a twenty-story water tank to clown around. We thought, "We're so cool. Look at us. Ta-da." We thought this was very courageous. While any potentially dangerous act does take a certain kind of courage, courage is much more than risk taking.

If courage was only risk taking, then those who risk their lives as stunt men or stunt women or those who risk their lives by drinking alcohol and driving would be the most courageous people in society. But real courage is not simply doing dangerous activities—it can instead come in many other forms. While an activity like rock climbing takes courage, courage can also be speaking what you believe in a situation where everyone else thinks another way or sharing your hopes and fears with a friend or standing up to someone who is being mean.

There is an old story that speaks to this inner courage. Many years ago, a group of warriors were going from village to village in Korea destroying houses and killing people. One day a village heard that this group was heading toward them, so they quickly gathered up their valuables and prepared to go hide in the mountains where they would be safe.

Everyone left the village except for one old priest, who insisted on staying in his temple. The villagers thought he was crazy to stay, but they could not get him to leave with them. When the warriors arrived and the leader learned that an old priest sat in the temple, the leader instantly rushed over. Storming through the doors, he walked forcefully up to the small man sitting calmly at the front of the temple. "Are you not afraid of me?" the warrior shouted. "Don't you know who I am? I'm the fiercest warrior in all the land. Why, I could cut your head off without batting an eye."

The priest looked up at the mighty warrior and responded, "And don't you know who I am? I could sit here and have you cut my head off without batting an eye." The priest did not threaten retaliation or try to talk the warrior out of killing him; he simply held his ground. And the story goes that it was the first time that the warrior met someone who was not afraid of him, and the priest's fearlessness and courage so moved him that he gave up his sword and took the priest as his teacher.

Now, this is just a story, but it speaks to a type of courage, one not simply based on risk taking or physical strength or mental knowledge. It speaks to a courage of spirit. The great activists in our history—Martin Luther King Jr.'s fight for civil rights in the United States, Mahatma Gandhi's work for independence in India, Mother Teresa of Calcutta's work to help the poor—had enormous courage, but their courage was driven by a deeper sense of purpose. At times it involved risking their lives, but this risk was only done as a way to serve something greater. In the story, the priest risked his life, but he did so as a way to stop future killing and devastation.

In my life, it has been the small acts that have actually taken the most courage—finding a job, telling a person that I would like to get to know him or her, working out a difficulty with a friend. The bigger acts, like walking and hitchhiking in far-off countries, actually did not seem to take much courage. It's not the big, dangerous acts that determine our courage, it's really the small, everyday acts that matter most.

The Town Ahead

Though there are difficult times in my life when it's extremely hard to feel grateful for anything, if I can find something to be grateful for, my mood usually improves. I learned this when, for several years, I hitchhiked quite a bit in the United States and Asia. I noticed that the more bored and anxious I got while standing on the side of the road, the fewer people stopped to give me a ride. Who wants to have boredom in their car for the next four hours, or anxiety, or worry? Satisfaction is a much better companion. So while standing on the side of the road, I practiced breathing, smiling, and enjoying the day. Even if it was raining or snowing, I tried to find something to enjoy. While standing there, I thought about the things I felt grateful for—my friends, having a warm coat on, the trees nearby. I could always think of something. Doing this not only helped me enjoy the day, but I also seemed to get more rides.

When we are not aware, we carry certain states of mind around with us. There is a story of a traveler who came upon an elderly man seated on a bench outside the entrance to a city. The traveler asked him, "What is this town ahead like?"

The elderly man replied, "First, tell me about the last town you visited."

"It was awful," replied the traveler. "The people were unfriendly, the food was horrible, the weather was bad."

"Well," said the man, "this next town will probably be about the same." The traveler then went gloomily on his way.

The next day another traveler walked by the same old man seated on the bench and asked about the village ahead. The elderly man again replied by asking him about the last town he visited.

This time the traveler responded, "Oh, it was lovely. The sunsets were beautiful, the people were fascinating, there were so many interesting places to visit."

The elderly man then replied, "The town ahead will most likely be the same as your last."

The man then went happily on his way.

When states of mind are not recognized, they color much of our experience. If we need gas, we only notice gas stations while driving down the street. If we are hungry, we mainly see restaurants.

Without any awareness or mindfulness, we are just like the traveler who brings his unpleasant state of mind with him wherever he goes, always thinking that his surroundings are the only source of his dissatisfaction. The more aware we are, the more we can see and let go of that which blocks the natural, open mind.

Gratitude Practice

Take some time to reflect on and write about what you feel grateful for in your life right now. If you are having a difficult time in your life and cannot immediately think of anything, please give it more effort. Maybe you are grateful that you have one friend in your life or one teacher that seems nice. Maybe you are grateful that you live in a friendly neighborhood or that you are in good health. Make a list of these things and try to remember this list throughout the day.

Kindness Is a Great Religion

For three and a half months one summer, I went on an environmental walk across Japan. I was with five Westerner friends, and we had arranged to walk for three months from Tokyo to Hiroshima with a group of Buddhist monks. But after two weeks with them, we had to split ways because of difficulties the two groups had. The result was that my friends and I were in Japan on our own, with little money, few contacts, and several months of walking to reach our destination. We knew that it would be difficult to survive in such an expensive country: an apple can cost two dollars, a cantaloupe can cost ten, and a hotel for the night would take up much of our funds.

So we learned the art of dumpster diving (which means to get food from dumpsters), and we slept in parks and train stations at night. It was not as bad as it may sound. The food from the dumpsters was always wrapped and fairly fresh and the parks were comfortable and safe to sleep in. There is little violence in Japan, and the homeless population in the parks at night were always quite welcoming. However, an occasional stay at a house or a temple where we could shower, wash our clothes, and get a hot meal was a real blessing.

Sometimes when we walked by a Buddhist temple, we asked if we could have housing for the night. We got a flat "no" almost all the time. It is really not in the Japanese custom to have surprise visitors as guests and the language barrier made communication more difficult. Though almost all the Buddhist temples we tried turned us down, the Catholic churches received us with open arms. There was usually a Westerner there who spoke English, and we were always provided with a hot meal, a shower, and a comfortable place to sleep.

Even if there was not a Westerner in residence, usually one of the Japanese priests spoke some English, and we spent many a night sharing stories until the wee hours. After several nice stays at such churches, I was asked by someone what religion I was. At first I hesitated, because I had not thought about it for awhile. After a few seconds, I responded, "Well, in California, I am more of a Buddhist. But now that I am in Japan, I am Catholic!" The person smiled, then tilted his head in confusion. I was partly making a joke, but not completely. I felt more heart and connection from my interactions with the Catholic church than I had from the Buddhist temples, and had I stayed in Japan longer I don't know whether it would have been at a Catholic church or a Buddhist monastery.

I learned through this experience that though I practice Buddhist techniques and read various Buddhist texts, it is the heart that really draws me. It reminds me of the statement by the Dalai Lama when he said, "My true religion is kindness." I learned in Japan that when it really comes down to it, my true religion is kindness as well, and that I practice and connect with traditions that help me cultivate such kindness.

Kindness permeates any true teaching. When someone helps us—offers us food when we are hungry, provides a caring ear, gives us needed guidance—we don't first ask them what religion they are before we receive their generosity. When kindness is present, where we come from, how we got there, and the rest does not matter. What matters is the richness that is shared. Some things are more important than any particular tradition, and this is the great tradition to which we all belong. So the next time someone asks me what religion I am, my most honest reply would be "kindness."

The heart of meditation practice, or any spiritual practice, is kindness. Writer and activist Bo Lozoff writes, "There is no spiritual practice more profound than being kind to one's family, neighbors, the cashier at the grocery store, an unexpected visitor, the con in the next cell, a stray dog or cat, or any other of the usually 'irrelevant' or 'invisible' beings who may cross our paths of a normal day. Certainly there are spiritual mysteries beyond description to explore, but as we mature, it becomes clear that those special experiences are only meaningful when they arise from and return to a life of ordinary kindness."

A Day of Kind Acts

For one day, focus on doing kind acts. Make breakfast for your friends or family, give a homeless person some money, hold the door for people as they enter a building. This is the day of kind acts, so let yourself go. You don't need to give away lots of money or start a new organization to feed the homeless, just do small acts of kindness. It may seem a little forced or phony, but remember, it is just for a day. After this day, you can do whatever you wish. But for this one day, kind acts are the focus.

Part-Time Buddhas

Any spiritual practice is not so much about becoming something that we are not, but allowing more of who we already are to unfold. Thich Nhat Hanh reminds us that we are all *part-time Buddhas*. We are all present and caring at times; the goal, he says, is to become a *full-time Buddha*. The practice is not about trying to be something that we are not, but is more about developing and nurturing what is already there. It is not an all-or-nothing game that we either win or lose at the end. We all have moments of joy and open-heartedness in our life. They may be seldom, but we all experience such moments.

Thich Nhat Hanh also says that it is as if we have seeds within us. Sometimes people water the seeds of our anger and fear, by calling us names or acting rudely, while other times they water our seeds of awareness and compassion by treating us with dignity and respect. We all have the seeds of awareness and compassion within us; the more we and others water those seeds, the more those qualities will be present.

Everyone cares about something. It may be something fleeting like money or a car, but the care is still there. The more we can see that care and speak to it, the more we will water the seeds of awareness in that person. It is not that we do not see their negative behavior or are oblivious to their destructive ways, it is that we don't *just* see that. We see that and more.

We all have the potential to live with awareness and compassion. The Buddha said that if it was not possible, it would be wrong to teach awareness practices. Mindfulness helps us remember to water the seeds of our true self, and to water those seeds in others. There's an old Indian saying, "The more you see God in others, the more others will see God in you." The more we see the great heart in others, the more people will see the great heart in us. In seeing and in watering the seeds of awareness and compassion in another, we water those seeds in ourselves.

Part Three

Meditations

Guided Mindfulness Meditation

As a young person, I first saw pictures in books of people meditating, and thought r-a-d-i-c-a-l. Something about it seemed so revolutionary, as if there was this whole other world to explore. I saw it as a way of stopping and facing life—facing fears, doubts, resentments, and finding in the process an inner strength. I also thought I might be able to gain some powers, like the ability to read people's minds or know what was going to be on a test. I wasn't sure, but I hoped that I would gain some kind of power that I could show off to friends. I had many different motivations in starting to practice meditation.

Meditation is a word that often makes us think of monks

or hermits in Asia, winding their legs around their back or

standing on their head. But meditation is not just for monks and hermits and we do not need to leave the country to do it. It is simply a way to pay attention and tune in to ourselves. More people practice meditation than we tend to think. To me, it is the same thing that a farmer might do in the morning, sitting down to have a cup of tea and staring out across his land, taking the time to settle his mind before tackling the day. Or what the performer does who sits quietly by herself, focusing on her breath to center herself before going on stage. Or what a weekend fisherman does when he spends a day on a quiet pond, focusing his mind on the water and waiting for fish to bite his line—people often go more to enjoy the stillness than to catch fish. Or what the person does who takes a short break to light up a cigarette, taking deep inhalations and exhalations as the smoke comes in and out of her lungs. In present day language, these are all forms of chilling, which, in many ways, is meditation. There are, of course, some meditations and ways of chilling that are healthier than others, but my point is that taking a break and focusing on the breath, or a lake, or land, are all types of meditation that are very much a part of our society. The meditations offered here are simply more structured types of paying attention.

One of the most common meditations is a silent mindfulness meditation. There are various versions of this practice, but the basic idea is to sit still and simply notice what happens—not controlling the process, not trying to figure anything out, but simply observing and noticing. Some traditions give very simple instructions, such as "just sit and be aware." Others focus more on posture or on keeping awareness focused at a particular place in the body. The following meditation uses awareness of the breath as the primary anchor or central place of focus. When you find yourself thinking about the past or the future, you use the breath to help focus and center you. You later begin to open to whatever experiences seem predominant, getting insight into the nature of life. This is why this meditation is sometimes called insight meditation. We begin to see more clearly the nature of our experience. This might not be making any sense, because talking about meditation is kind of like talking about swimming. It can help a little, but we only know for ourselves by trying it.

The basis of this practice is a deep listening to your body and mind. There is no need to control or fix anything. Instead, simply enjoy the simplicity and beauty of life. It is a time to stop, to listen, and to simply be.

You may be wondering:

What do I do first?

Find a time and place where you feel comfortable and will not be interrupted.

How do I sit?

You can either sit on a pillow or cushion or in a chair. If you sit on a cushion, sit with your legs crossed, and your back straight but not rigid. Sit so that one leg is folded in front of the other. It is often easiest to first fold one leg and then fold the other, so that both your knees touch the floor. At first your knees may rise off the floor because you are not accustomed to sitting on the floor. It may be helpful to add an extra cushion or two so that you are a little higher off the ground. This can help your back to be straight and your legs to rest on the floor. After practicing for awhile, you will become more limber. Most important is that your back be straight.

If you use a chair, sit with your back straight and your feet on the floor, with your hands folded gently in your lap. When using a chair, I find it easier to sit on the edge of the chair so that my posture is upright. Sitting on couches or other more cushioned chairs can be more difficult because it is easy to lean back and get too relaxed and fall asleep. Most importantly, experiment and see what works for you.

What posture is best?

It's not like there is one perfect meditation posture, but it is helpful if your posture supports alertness and attention, without being rigid.

What do I do with the rest of my body?

You can fold your hands in your lap or gently place them on your knees. It is common to want to fiddle or play with your hands when sitting down. Wherever you put your hands, try to keep them in that same place for the meditation period. Try to keep them as still as possible. A still body makes it easier to concentrate.

Your head should tilt downward just a little, as if you are looking out to sea. Your posture should support awareness and attentiveness, but it should not be tight or rigid. Let your posture be relaxed, yet alert. Sit with the dignity of a king or queen. Sit with respect.

I like to gently close my eyes to meditate, but if that seems weird you can keep them open. If you do, it is best to find one place on the floor or wall to concentrate on; otherwise, your attention is likely to wander around the room.

What if I my legs or back starts to hurt?

First notice the pain. Unless the pain is really strong, see if you can relax around the pain. By this, I mean bring a calm attention to it. But if it feels like the pain is too much, then try to adjust your posture so that you are more comfortable. Though the intention is to sit still for the meditation period, meditation is not about causing yourself more pain. So if you need to move, do so slowly and with awareness.

Keep experimenting to see what posture works for you and realize that some discomfort is inevitable.

How long should I meditate?
See what feels right. Maybe try ten to fifteen minutes at first. You want to do it long enough so that you get a taste of it, but not push yourself so much that it feels like a drag. Start small, then gradually build at a pace that feels right.

What should I wear?
Currently, navy blue is in fashion among people who meditate. Also, vests are in, turtlenecks are out. Whatever you do, don't wear yellow. It's considered too showy. (I'm joking. Wear whatever is comfortable.) Also, if you sit on a cushion, it is best to take your shoes off (seriously).

What do I do next?
It will be easiest to read the following guided meditation very slowly to yourself, then close your eyes afterwards and give it a try. You may want to read this meditation several times before closing your eyes to practice. You can also record this meditation on a tape and play it back.

Take your time. There is no rush. Read the meditation silently to yourself as many times as you need before giving it a try.

As you sit down and close your eyes, it may feel a little unusual at first. Notice what it feels like to sit here. You may notice that sounds become more evident. Notice all the different sounds around you. Maybe you hear the sound of traffic outside, or the sound of a refrigerator, or the sound of your own heart beating. Simply notice what sounds are predominant.

Next take a couple of deep breaths into your belly. Let your breath fill your belly with air on the inhalation, then let your whole body relax on the exhalation.

Now let your breath come and go naturally, and feel your breath in your body. Notice how you experience your breath. As you feel your breath, gently allow your body to relax with each inhalation and with each exhalation. With each breath, let your body soften a little more. Let your mind become a little more still.

Let your body be soft and open but also upright and dignified. Your shoulders, jaw, belly, all soft. As the breath comes in and out, allow your body to come into a natural and relaxed state. Let each breath soothe you, refresh you, nourish you. Like drinking cold water on a hot summer day.

The breath has its own natural rhythm. The belly rises with each inhalation and falls with each exhalation. The chest expands with each inhalation and contracts with *each exhalation. Sensations can also be felt at the nostrils as the breath moves in and out. Notice the various places you feel the breath in your body.*

Notice the rhythm of the breath. How each breath is unique. There is no need to "try" to breathe. The breath comes and goes all on its own. Let your attention rest on the breath. See how it comes and goes like waves on the ocean. If the breath is short, let it be short. If it is long, let it be long. Simply let the breath be as it is.

Notice how each breath has a beginning, a middle, and an end. Watch the pattern of the breath in the body.

The belly, soft. The mind, clear. The heart, open. Your mind open and spacious, like a vast blue sky. Notice how thoughts come and go all by themselves. They arise, exist for a moment, then pass away, like clouds in this vast sky. Whatever thoughts arise, simply let them be. Let thoughts come, let them be, and let them go.

Body soft. Shoulders soft. Eyes soft.

Notice the joy and magic in just one breath. The breath allows you to open, to listen, to know. Coming more in tune with your body and mind. Experience each moment anew. Each moment just as it is.

Follow the inner rhythms of your breath. Life unfolding as it will. Nothing to change or condemn. Just moment-to-moment change. Mind clear, body soft, heart open.

More instructions on this type of meditation can be found in *Seeking the Heart of Wisdom* by Jack Kornfield and Joseph Goldstein, *Wherever You Go, There You Are* by Jon Kabat-Zinn, or *A Gradual Awakening* by Stephen Levine.

The Many Faces of Meditation

So you decide to give meditation a try. What might happen? Who knows? You may enjoy it, or you may not. But likely you will have days when you enjoy it and days when you don't. The following meditation pictures are not of what *should* happen, but simply what you may experience.

There will likely be days when you seem to go back and forth and find yourself greatly enjoying it one moment then not at all the next. One moment you think that the practice is the greatest thing ever; you can never imagine not doing it. Other moments, it is not so pleasant and you think that you will never do it again. There are times when we seem to jump back and forth between two extremes as we try to decide whether we should continue with it. You **111** may have noticed this same tendency when you first started playing a sport or an instrument. The first day, you think that it is the greatest thing on earth, but the next day you think it is awful. In the beginning of any practice, we often jump back and forth between these views.

Such a meditation may go something like **Figure One** on the facing page.

Other times, the last thing we want to do is meditate. We wake up in the morning from a long night, roll out of bed, glance at our meditation area, and think "No way." We got into an argument with our friend the previous night, and we don't want to sit with the frustration and anger that we feel. No way, we think. Forget it. During such times, we start running through our top-ten list of reasons not to practice:

10. I've got better things to do.
9. It can be boring.
8. It's a waste of time.
7. You never know what will happen.
6. Ignorance is bliss.

5. My life may change.
4. My life may not change.
3. Isn't *The Simpsons* on?
2. I will miss out on something else.

And number 1:

My friends will think it is stupid.

And there are many, many more. They may even be really good reasons. They may be reasons you decide later to act on. But if you are in the check-it-out period and have

Figure One: Jumping Back and Forth Between Two Extremes

The Many Faces of Meditation

decided to give it a try for a few weeks, it can be useful to do it anyway.

At times meditation can seem like the hardest thing in the world. Sometimes at very difficult times in my practice, I would think "at least I am not meditating now." Meditation was so difficult that I became more grateful for the rest of my life when I was not meditating. My mind would not stay still even for a second and it seemed like a hopeless cause. Practicing when we do not feel like it can be difficult, but at times it can be worthwhile. Sometimes our state of mind will remain the same for our meditation time, but often it will change. We may at first notice anger, the resistance to doing it, then sadness over an argument the previous night, then fear over what we said, then worry over what our friend thinks of us now, then righteousness about the way we acted, then remorse, and finally we may experience care for our friend and realize how much we value his or her friendship.

Though it seems like only one state of mind is present, often there are multiple levels to our experience. We may go into a meditation angry at a friend, and come out of it realizing how much we care about him or her. We never know, but any awareness we can bring to our experience certainly helps.

We may have meditations that go something like **Figure Two** on the facing page.

Figure Two: Multiple Levels to Our Experience

Minute 1 — What was I thinking when I decided to do this?

Minute 2 — I must have been sitting here for twenty minutes

Minute 3 — My leg hurts.

Minute 4 — I'm thirsty. Maybe I should get up and get a drink

Minute 5 — I am never doing this again.

Minute 6 — This is ridiculous.

Minute 7 — Oh, that was a nice thought.

Minute 8 — Breathing in. Breathing out.

Minute 9 — Calm.

The Many Faces of Meditation

Other times we feel much ease and calm, and it seems there is a natural peace that comes over us. It is not a lot of effort or struggle to be present. We experience each moment coming and going and we feel ourselves a part of a beautiful flow. It does not even feel like effort. It feels like a complete joy and we simply are in the great flow of life. We wonder how we could have previously struggled. All is calm and peaceful. It is simply a joy to practice.

Such a meditation may go something like **Figure Three** on the facing page.

However, after such a meditation the next time we may think, "Boy, I have sure mastered this meditation stuff," and we expect our next time to be the same, or even better. We may even think that we have mastered the art of living all together. *In only a few meditations,* we may think, *I have rid myself of all fear, anger, and doubt. That was not so hard. I guess some of us are just naturals.* However, though the seeds of anger, doubt, and sadness were not present in one sitting, it does not mean that they are completely gone. While it is wonderful that we had a deep and pleasant meditation, they do not always go so smoothly. While the seeds were not present, they still remain in our consciousness and can arise again when the conditions are there. Slowly, through understanding and awareness we can turn

Figure Three: All Is Calm and Peaceful

The Many Faces of Meditation

these seeds, these difficulties, that once caused us suffering into seeds that nurture our compassion and understanding. But it takes time and work. If we try to hold on to a particular state and think "it will always be this way" we will likely be disappointed.

We think if it was peaceful the last time, it should be that way again, but unfortunately (or fortunately) it does not work that way. Each meditation has its own flavor and there is no way to guess beforehand what it will be like.

Such a meditation may go something like **Figure Four** on the facing page.

Later we may feel like we are getting the hang of it. We are able to sit still for longer periods of time and feel some sense of ease. However, we may realize that our mind can go off on pleasant thoughts just as much as unpleasant ones. We may find ourselves lost in cool thoughts about the powers we will get from meditation or how we can impress our friends. If you do not think you have such thoughts of wanting power and control, you are in for a surprise. It is all in there. Though we may think that we are above or beyond certain thoughts, they can still arise and catch us off guard. Big surprise! The people who say that they only think holy thoughts are the people I most distrust. While holy thoughts are lovely, there is usually more under the surface for us to see.

Figure Four: Each Meditation Has Its Own Flavor

The Many Faces of Meditation

We might have a meditation like **Figure Five** on the facing page.

Often, however, meditation is simply sitting with ourselves and gradually learning more patience, care, and wisdom. We don't always have big flashes of light or tremendous mind-blowing insights, but very slowly we are deepening our ability to concentrate and learn more about ourselves. There are no great fireworks or huge revelations; it is simply a gradual sensitizing and awakening. It may seem like nothing is happening, but if we look back over several months of working with these techniques, we will notice changes. We will see that we are a little more patient with a difficult friend or a little less likely to react in anger when we are upset. Sitting in meditation we gradually develop more understanding and patience with our own mind and body.

Such meditations may go something like **Figure Six** on page 122.

Figure Six: We Gradually Develop More Understanding and Patience

Meditation Hints

The breath is a very good subject of meditation. We can be aware of the breath in various ways. We can have a more expansive awareness of the breath and as we breathe in we simply know that we are breathing in; as we breathe out, we know that we breathe out. We can use a general awareness, following the various sensations as the breath comes in and goes out. As your awareness becomes more aligned with your breath, you also may find it helpful to focus on the area where you feel the breath the easiest. The most common place is the rise and fall of the belly or the in-and-out sensations of the breath at the nostrils. Notice which of these areas naturally draws your attention, and then stay with that area as your primary focus. This is the place you will return to when your mind wanders. If it is helpful, you can say silently in your mind the word "rising" as the belly rises and "falling" as the belly falls, or "in" as the breath goes in through the nostrils, then "out" as the breath goes out. This may help you stay more in touch with your breath. No one place is better than another, simply notice where the sensations are most easily felt.

If you focus on your abdomen rising and falling, you are focusing on the sensation of the movement. It is not about controlling or visualizing the breath, but staying attentive to the movement as the abdomen rises and falls. The body breathes all by itself without our effort; we simply need to pay attention to the process.

The breath can be a source of great nourishment. Try not breathing for awhile, and the breath will take on a whole new meaning. Numerous martial arts teach that awareness of the breath is the central art of their practice; it is what weaves through all of their different forms. It is helpful to look upon the breath as something that is nourishing and refreshing, like a cold glass of water on a hot day, or the warmth of a fire when coming in from the cold, or as water splashed on one's face from a cool stream. There is a particular rhythm to the breath, a flow. It comes and goes like the waves on an ocean. See if you can become attuned to that inner rhythm.

Wanderlust

After a minute or so focusing on the breath, you may think, "Wow, this is fairly simple. It is different than I thought. I remember watching that movie where a guy meditated. What a cool movie. There was that actor . . ." These are called associated thoughts and they are endless. One thought can lead to another thought and another. . . . At this point, very gently allow your breath to again become predominant. You can use mental noting by making a silent and soft note in the back of your mind, "thinking, thinking," before returning to your primary object. Such noting is not a judging of the experience but a naming of it. The note should be very soft and light. It is not a heavy handed slap, but a gentle guiding. It is a way of acknowledging the truth **125** of the moment and using the breath to align your awareness with the present moment. A soft, kind note is most useful.

If a car drives by or if we notice a smell, we can note them too, as "hearing, hearing" or "smelling, smelling." Or if there is particular predominant state of mind such as joy or anger, we can note the experience as "joy, joy" or "anger, anger." It is easy to take it personally when fear or anger arises and think, "Oh, this is bad. I'm such a bad meditator. I fail at everything I try. It is hopeless. I'll never become . . ." So rather than personalizing it, we simply note it for what it is. Anger is present, fear is present, love is present, joy is present. Whatever is occurring can be seen for what it is. Even if it is something strong like hatred, we can acknowledge it, bow to it, and realize that this is fertilizer to help us develop more understanding and compassion. No matter what the state is, we can be assured that almost everyone in the world has experienced something similar. We are never alone, in both our struggles or our successes.

Noting is a powerful tool for staying with our direct experience, whether it is pleasant or unpleasant. If love or happiness arises, they too can be seen and noted. By noting we are helping to meet whatever arises with understanding and mindfulness. Noting is a wonderful tool, and like all tools there will be certain meditations and times in our practice when it seems very useful and other times when it is not so needed. The goal is not to find the right name for an experience but to open to the moment as it is.

You may notice that when your attention is off your primary object, judgment will arise, such as "You messed up again. You're off your primary object. You're no good at this." If your mind judges your wandering as bad or wrong, simply notice the judgment itself as just another thought. You can note it softly as "judging, judging." The conditioned response of the mind is often to judge. Though our intention is to have a nonjudgmental awareness, judgment will still arise. Judgment can be seen as what it is: just another thought that arises and passes. You can even begin to expect it. *I notice that my awareness is off my primary object again, judgment will be coming any moment now. There it is!* You can simply acknowledge and notice it without reinforcing more judgment.

The Breath, Right

Sometimes ten or fifteen minutes go by and you notice that you have forgotten all about your breath. You wake up and remember, "Oh yeah, I'm meditating. The breath, right." It does not matter how long you were away, simply allow your breath to again become predominant. It is not a matter of roughly yanking your awareness back to the breath, but instead simply allowing the breath to be in the foreground, to be noticeable. Other thoughts, sounds, and sensations will still arise in the background. You will come back to the present moment a million more times in your life if you are lucky, so you might as well make such **128** moments gentle and joyful.

The breath is a good primary object to use since it is continually changing and brings us back to our direct experience. However, the goal is not to become a good breather. Meditation is more about cultivating awareness. This means not just awareness of the breath but an awareness that includes our thoughts, feelings, states of mind, the truths of life, and the sense pathways of hearing, tasting, touching, smelling, and seeing.

The breath is used to anchor you in the present moment so that you can then expand your awareness to include whatever is predominant. It is helpful initially to have an anchor, a primary object, to come back to. Eventually as concentration develops, your awareness can expand to include whatever is predominant, be it the breath, sounds, feelings, or thoughts. Before we can bring our awareness to other areas we usually need a certain amount of concentration, which awareness on the breath helps to develop.

The mind is amazingly creative and is a great problem solver. It is a wonderful tool, but at times we need a rest from the active habits of the mind. Meditation is a time to let the body and mind settle and restore themselves. We don't need to figure anything out or solve some big problem. It is a time to let the mind settle, let it rest. Awareness of the breath helps the mind focus on something other than the exam coming up, the friend we are angry at, and other mind stuff. The breath deepens as our awareness is directed toward it, allowing both the body and mind to experience some ease and rest.

When the mind begins to wander and worry, causing us to lose touch with the present moment, we use the breath to remind ourselves to rest, to soften. The breath reminds us of the ease of being that is our natural state.

Exploration

As your concentration on your breath deepens, you may want to expand your awareness to include other parts of your experience. At first it may seem kind of mechanical—"I'm noticing my breath, okay." But you do not have to fight off thoughts, sounds, feelings, or whatever else arises. As you notice your awareness settled with your breath, you may want to expand your awareness to include other experiences that arise. You may focus on a sensation in your body or a thought or feeling or whatever is predominant. If when doing this your mind wanders, as it inevitably will, and you lose focus, come back to the breath as a way to center yourself. The breath is home base.

It is kind of like learning to play a musical instrument. If you want to learn to play the guitar, you need to find a **131** teacher or begin by yourself and learn how each string sounds. Initially, you need to focus on learning the sounds of the guitar. If you try to join a band while you are just learning to play, you will get overwhelmed and never learn how your sounds interact with the rest of the band. But once you know the cords and can play a few tunes, you can then play in a band and not just focus on your particular instrument but learn to play along with all these other instruments. In the same way, the breath is used as the anchor, but your awareness can expand to include other experiences that arise.

At first meditation instructions can seem a little dry, like you are simply following a cooking recipe: *Do this, don't do that*. But the directions are there to get you going. Later you can begin to trust yourself more. The directions come more from your own heart and experience than from anything you read in a book. The instructions are tools to help you see for yourself what is true.

Most importantly, keep an attitude of openness and exploration. You do not need to try and figure everything out in your first meditation. Watch the tendency to make it very complicated. It is not. Meditation is for your own benefit and joy. It is not always fun or easy, but it is helpful to have an attitude of ease and lightness. So much of our daily life is spent worrying; meditation is a time to rest. It is a time to be easy and gentle with yourself, a time to enjoy just being alive.

Learning to Surf

During meditation you will notice that your awareness jumps from here to there. Sometimes it is on the breath, sometimes it is focused on sensations in the body, and a great deal of the time it is thinking—thinking about all kinds of things—what you will do tomorrow, what a friend said yesterday, a new CD you want to buy. Thoughts or subjects may arise that we realize we need to think about more and wisely reflect on. One of the cool aspects of meditation is that it helps us to see what areas in our life need more attention. Rather than think about this subject the entire meditation (though you can if you want—we are all free agents) it is often best to simply make a note of it, and to give the subject or thought more reflection after the **133** meditation period. If during a meditation you remember that you need to study for a test, rather than plan your study schedule or worry about the test, acknowledge that you need to take care of this soon, then continue with the meditation.

There is a difference between thinking about or visualizing the breath and experiencing it directly. In meditation we directly touch the breath, not as thought but as sensation. We notice the changing sensations in each inhalation and exhalation, the changes in pressure and sensation as the breath moves through the body. By directly experiencing the breath, we can receive our moment-to-moment experience as it arises and passes. This direct contact helps us to get out of our *thoughts* about ourselves and into our *experience* of ourselves.

Meditation involves noticing thoughts. We see how they arise and pass away. Thoughts arise uninvited. We don't ask ourselves to think of something. Thoughts think themselves; they have their own momentum. We could say to our mind, "Stop. Please stop now," but this never works. There is an openness of mind that can see thoughts clearly. When the mind is spacious, we can see thoughts arise and pass away, kind of like clouds passing through a vast blue sky.

As we practice we see that there are various levels of mind. There is the monkey mind that bounces here and there without control, but there is also what is called Big Mind or spacious mind. This is the mind that sees clearly, that sees directly. Big Mind is the mind that is open and clear, that is attentive and receptive. This is the mind that sees with wisdom and compassion.

We cannot experience Big Mind from trying to stop our thoughts, but only from developing more space for them to arise and pass. Some people think that if they try hard enough, they can subdue all thoughts. But this is hard, if not impossible. The third Zen Patriarch said, "When you try to stop activity to achieve passivity, your very effort fills you with activity." Thoughts arise and pass away like everything else. Our effort to stop them just creates more. Rather than try to fight them, give them room to arise and pass away. There is a flow that we can begin to tune into. This flow cannot be controlled, but we can find harmony in it; we can learn to ride its waves. We cannot stop thoughts but we can learn to see them clearly. As someone else put it: "We cannot stop the waves, but we can learn to surf."

Openness to What Is

As you become more aware of your mind, you notice all kinds of thoughts. Sometimes the thoughts are difficult to see. Thoughts of wanting something a friend has, of causing injury to someone who has hurt you, or of ways to coerce or lie to get your way will all arise. Almost everyone has such thoughts at times. However, there is a difference between the thought and the action. Acknowledging such thoughts can deepen your compassion and wisdom by giving you a chance to see them directly. Without awareness, you habitually act on such thoughts and only realize their harmful nature once you feel the effects some time later. Acting on such thoughts creates a chain of suffering **136** that causes needless pain and injury. However, to begin to gain access to these tendencies, you must be willing to see what is there. This requires a sense of welcoming, a willingness to allow and accept whatever thoughts or feelings arise. There is a certain power in acknowledging the truth of the moment. The truth can be that rage or greed is present, but in the acknowledging of it you get a little more breathing room, a little more space to understand and to respond wisely.

This does not mean you relish in your thoughts to cause pain or to cheat someone, but to give these thoughts room to be seen and touched with understanding and then to let them go, to not encourage them. Acceptance is the starting point since, in essence, you cannot change anything that you do not first accept. There is an art to noticing and accepting certain difficult states without feeding them or encouraging their pattern.

Many people think acceptance means repressing bad thoughts: *Throw all those bad thoughts under the carpet and everything will be great.* It is similar to our ideas about fearlessness. Many people see fearlessness as a mind that fear never enters. They strive to build a big wall between themselves and fear. To be fearless, however, does not mean that fear never enters the mind; it means that it arises but we do not habitually fight it or get overwhelmed and act on it. If we try to resist fear, we become afraid of fear. We say, "I hope fear does not arise. I will try to stop it." This is not freedom from fear; this is fear of fear. Freedom from fear is to see fear directly and know that, just like all states of mind, it arises and passes away. Though it huffs and puffs while it is present, it too is temporary. When we have less care whether or not fear arises, we are closer to that freedom. Rather than a freedom *from* fear, it seems to be more like learning freedom *with* fear. This is not to say that I do not get absolutely frightened at times or that fear never overwhelms me. It does. Sometimes, too, fear has a message behind it, telling us that we need to pay attention to what we are doing or that we are in a dangerous situation that we need to leave.

Acceptance involves making space for our experience. The Zen teacher Suzuki Roshi said that if you want to control a wild animal, you should give it a large space in which to roam. The more we try to push away experience or keep it locked up, the more control it has over us. Acceptance creates space for experience so we can see it clearly. So if fear arises, we do not need to pretend it is not there or become overwhelmed by it and withdraw. We can acknowledge it as the truth of the moment. The tendency is to either repress or fight our experience. There is, however, a middle way of opening and accepting. We can notice and acknowledge thoughts without getting lost in their story. By acknowledging difficult states of mind we are not encouraging or reinforcing them, but are rather bringing the light of mindfulness to them. The Vietnamese monk and poet Thich Nhat Hanh writes, "To practice mindfulness of the mind does not mean not to be agitated. It means that when we are agitated, we know that we are agitated. Our agitation has a good friend in us, and that is mindfulness."

Painful memories from one's past can also arise. It is important to acknowledge the truth of such experiences. Seeing that everything arises and passes does not mean that we deny our thoughts and feelings. Painful memories can start a deep healing process that one may need to consult a therapist, friend, or teacher to work with more deeply. A deep healing can take place just in our honest opening to the intensity of such an experience. We must listen deeply to ourselves to hear what we need for healing to take place. Nothing can be excluded from this process. Meditation is one of many tools that can be useful, but only our intuition knows what other tools we need at a particular time.

While at times it is hard to sit with the difficult experiences, our heart is strengthened by the truth. Everything can be investigated. When we sit in meditation, we sit with the power of awareness. The great Indian social activist Gandhi called his autobiography *The Story of My*

Experiments with Truth. All of our lives are experiments with truth. Whether we meditate or not, we still face the same challenges. Meditation and other awareness exercises simply provide us with tools to face these challenges. One of my teachers says, "It is hard to meditate, but it is even harder not to." A practice that cultivates awareness is not easy because we continue to see those places in us that need healing; however, a life without awareness is much more painful.

Walking Meditation

There are many types of meditations. The meditations in the next several sections use different areas of focus and different phrases. It is not like one type of meditation is better than another; it is about finding what works for you. And it can change over time depending on what you need. But all these practices are ways to cultivate awareness, compassion, and wisdom, which is the heart of all meditation practice. One type that you may want to try is walking meditation.

Have you ever noticed that when you are upset or stressed, if you go for a walk it can help settle your mind? Walking is a great way to get some exercise and to let the body and mind slow down a bit. It can be a time to reflect and to see important issues more clearly.

While it can help to simply go for a walk, there are also walking meditations that help build concentration and relaxation. Walking meditation is one of many movement meditations that help bring our sitting meditation practice into daily life. The principle is the same as sitting practice: to be present for what we are doing and experiencing in the moment.

There are various ways to practice walking meditation. One way is to find a path about ten to thirty paces in length. This space will be your walking path. Begin by walking very slowly. Let your hands rest at your sides. Relax your shoulders and jaw. Walk with dignity and gentleness. Pay attention to each step that you take. Notice the change of pressure and sensations as you walk. Bring your attention to each footstep, noticing how each step involves a lifting, moving, and placing. Walk with ease and joy. Gently bring your attention back to your body and your footsteps whenever your mind wanders.

If it is helpful, you can note quietly to yourself "lifting" as the foot lifts, "moving" as you move the foot, then "placing" as your foot touches the ground. Depending on the speed you are walking, you may just want to note "Lifting, placing" or even just "placing" if you are moving at a good pace. Use such noting if it is useful, but if it seems to get in the way, then let it go and simply be with the experience of walking.

Another way to do walking meditation is to coordinate your steps with your breath. In this practice, walk a little slower than normal and notice how many steps you take while inhaling and how many steps you take while exhaling. You may notice that you take two steps each inhalation and three steps each exhalation. Don't try to control the breath. There is no "right" breath sequence. Listen to your body, and find what your natural rhythm is.

Once you have found your rhythm, coordinate your footsteps to various words. Two words that you can use are "calm" and "ease." Say these silently to yourself as you walk. So if you take two steps on your inhalation, you silently say "calm" as each foot touches the ground. Then on the exhalation say "ease," on each step. So it would go, "calm, calm, ease, ease, ease."

You can also use the word "yes" with the inhalation and "thank you" on the exhalation. If we have not seen a good friend for many years and then he or she shows up at our door, we immediately think "yes" to ourselves because we are so happy to see that person. Then we feel so thankful that they are with us. In this meditation, we practice doing this with life. If we notice a beautiful tree or colorful bird or vibrant flower, we welcome it in the same way. We say, "Yes, thank you." So if you take two steps with each inhalation and three with each exhalation, this meditation would go, "yes,

yes," for the two steps on your inhalation and "thank you, thank you, thank you," for the three steps of your exhalation.

You can also create your own sayings, depending on what you want to cultivate in your life at that time. During walking meditation, if your attention is drawn toward a flower or a cat, stop and be present with it, then gently bring your attention back to your walking meditation.

It is best to do walking meditation on a quiet path in nature, but it can be practiced anywhere. You can do it as you walk to a friend's house or to school, or when waiting for a bus.

Thich Nhat Hanh offers us the following *Gatha* for beginning walking meditation:

> The mind can go in a thousand directions
> But on this beautiful path, I walk in peace.
> With each step, a gentle wind blows
> With each step, a flower blooms.

This is a time to let our worries go and simply be with the wonder of walking. Some of the simplest actions can be the most enjoyable.

For more information on walking meditation, please consult *The Long Road Turns to Joy: A Guide to Walking Meditation* by Thich Nhat Hanh.

Strength

Trusting in our own strength is not easy. We all have an idea of how we would live if we really trusted ourselves. Learning to trust in our strength shows us that we can be with the various states of mind and body that can arise. This strength is not an I'm-stronger-than-you attitude, rather it is tapping into the strength to which we all have access. This strength does not overpower others, but encourages others to feel their strength as well. It is the strength that we each share just in being alive.

Much of the challenge in life is learning to trust ourselves, to trust in our ability to persevere and thrive. Trusting that we can learn, that we can open ourselves, that we can see the beauty even in times of great hardship, takes a **145** deep commitment. One of the greatest inhibitors to any practice is doubt—doubt that we can fully be ourselves, doubt that we have the inner resources we need. Nature offers images that can help us remember our ability to trust. Symbols in nature such as a mountain, a lake, or the sky can be used as images that reflect our essential nature. The earth serves as a valuable reminder of the positive qualities within each of us.

At one point the Buddha was sitting in the forest meditating and was bombarded by intense feelings of doubt, greed, and hatred. Powerful images and forces arose to make him question his commitment and trust in his practice. It was his most difficult night. He responded by putting his hand down on the earth and calling on the power and strength of the earth. He called upon the earth to be the witness of his diligence and purity of heart. Soon after, the forces that troubled him subsided and he once again felt peaceful and strong. Calling upon the earth for guidance and support is an ancient practice that numerous traditions continue to use. We can ask the earth for guidance whenever we need help remembering our strength.

The following mountain meditation uses the image of the mountain as a way to help us tap into and trust the inherent strength in each of us. This strength is not about being physically fit or having a big vocabulary, rather it is the strength of the heart that can shine through in any situation. This meditation focuses on seeing and trusting the strength in each of us.

In this meditation, picture your favorite mountain that you have seen either in person or in a picture. If nothing comes to mind, use the image of your ideal mountain. The mountain might be filled with trees or it might be barren or full of snow. There could be a lake at the bottom or a valley. Use whatever image of a mountain that seems most useful.

Mountain Meditation

Find a comfortable sitting position. Let your body take an upright but relaxed position. Then gently let your eyes close.

Begin to picture a mountain. Notice the strength of this mountain, how long it has survived, how it welcomes all visitors, yet remains calm and strong.

Bring this image of the mountain into your own body. Sit with the strength of a mountain. Notice the underlying stillness, the underlying strength, that is there. Notice your capacity to be with whatever arises. Solid. Steady. Rains come, the sun shines, friendly and not-so-friendly animals come to visit, but the mountain remains.

Sense the underlying strength that is present. Everything arises and passes away in its own time and rhythm.

147

Trust in your own strength. Not the strength that dominates but the strength of presence, the strength to be with the moment just as it is.

Sit like a mountain, solid yet open. Each breath deepening your feeling of strength and ease. The breath coming and going in its own natural rhythm. Each inhalation deepening your feeling of strength, each exhalation feeling steady. Sitting with patience and equanimity. Solid, strong, easy.

Being open to whatever the moment offers. Trusting in your own strength and your ability to be present

Let everything come and go. Being with the moment-to-moment change. Solid, steady, strong.

Trust in the strength of the mountain, in your own strength. The strength to be present, to be with the moment just as it is. No force, no strain, simply allowing your strength to be present.

Thoughts and feelings come and go, but the mountain remains. Solid, strong, steady.

The Body

Our bodies often do not get the respect they deserve. We ask a lot of them. Too often we ask for much, but give very little in return. We demand, but often do not listen.

Some of us relate to our bodies in continual disapproval. We are disappointed that our hair is not a certain way, that we are too thin or too fat, too tall or too short, our head is too big or too small, our eyes should be blue rather than green. Our bodies can be places that become carrying cases for our disapproval and grief.

The following body awareness meditation brings a gentle, caring awareness to the body. Rather than telling the body how it is not right, we bring our awareness to the level of sensation in the body. We tune into it. We listen to it. **149**

This awareness does not attempt to modify or change the body, but to treat the body with a gentleness. We soften the muscles that have become tense, we touch with kindness that which we have often tightened and resisted. We begin to relate to the body with a type of gentleness. Bringing this gentle awareness to the body, we begin to both come to a greater experiential understanding of the body, and learn to treat it with respect and kindness.

The body in our culture is, on the one hand, given an enormous amount of attention. We spend billions of dollars a year to adorn the body with particular clothing and perfume. We dress it well and are encouraged to believe that *we are* our body. But in another way, the body is given very little direct attention. Though we do much to work with the outer appearance of the body, we do little to touch the body directly. We can see the shape and features of our body by looking in a mirror, but we can only get a sense of what it feels like by bringing our attention directly to the body. Is our belly tight or soft? What are the sensations at our chest? What are the sensations at the bottom of our feet? What does our jaw feel like? Touching the body at the level of sensation is to directly experience the body, not as a thought or image, but as a living system.

One of the primary practices in meditation is awareness of the body. This includes awareness of the breath, body postures, and the fact that the nature of the body is to change and decay. Though the body eventually decays and returns back to the earth, we can learn a great deal from having a body. Our body can become a part of our learning laboratory, a means to remind us of the power of mindfulness and love.

In this meditation, we explore the various sensations of the body. We are not thinking about the body, but directly touching it. Through this direct contact we get to know the body better. We learn to relate to it with kindness and care. For this meditation, you may choose to lie down. You may also want to experiment with this meditation before going to bed at night.

Body Awareness Meditation

Find a comfortable position and gently let your eyes close.

Let the breath come and go as it will. Allow the breath to be just as it is.

Next bring your attention to your body. What does your body feel like? Notice the various feelings that arise as you tune into your body. Nothing is right or wrong, simply notice what arises as you bring awareness to your body.

Let the attention you bring to your body be kind. Relate to the body with gratitude and appreciation, as if it were something very precious and mysterious. Bring a gentle awareness to the mystery of the body.

Begin by noticing the muscles in your face, then soften those muscles. Soften your eyes. Relax the jaw. Then move your awareness to your shoulders. Notice what your shoulders feel like and see if you can soften the muscles in the shoulders. Then let your awareness move down to your belly. Take a couple of deep breaths and begin to soften the muscles of the belly. Allow the belly to be open and relaxed. Then feeling your feet, notice how your feet feel. Let the muscles in your feet relax.

Now feel your whole body sitting here. The pressure of the body sitting on the floor or in the chair. Be aware of your whole body. If there is any place that seems to need attention, let your awareness focus there. Bring a feeling of calm and ease to this area. Be like a researcher on a voyage to a new land. Look around and notice what you see.

Treat the body with kindness and respect. Take care of it. Listen to it. Send care and awareness to any part of your body that needs attention. Touch the body with a gratefulness, an acceptance.

Soften all the muscles of the body. Let your body rest.
152 *Let it come back to its relaxed natural state.*

The body soft and open. Each breath bringing a sense of ease and well-being. Moment-to-moment change, moment-to-moment healing.

The breath full. The body open. The mind clear.

Gatha Meditation

This meditation works with the *Gatha* developed by Thich Nhat Hanh that reads:

Breathing in, I calm my body.
Breathing out, I smile.
Breathing in, I dwell in the present moment,
Breathing out, I know it is a wonderful moment.

Find a comfortable way to sit on a cushion or chair. On the first inhalation give complete attention to the in-breath and say the first line of the *Gatha* silently to yourself. Then give complete attention to the out-breath and say the **154** second line. On your next inhalation shorten the first line just to the word "Calm." On the out-breath just say the word "Smile."

Breathing in, I calm my body.
Breathing out, I smile.
Calm.
Smile.

Allow five, ten, or fifteen in-and-out breaths before moving to the second part of the *Gatha*. Let the first part sink in before moving on. The second part of the *Gatha* is used just as the first part.

Breathing in, I dwell in the present moment,
Breathing out, I know it is a wonderful moment.
Present moment.
Wonderful moment.

This is a simple meditation that can be done anywhere, any time of day. The smiling and calming of the first part helps us to stop and come back home. The second part then enables us to touch the joy of the present moment.

Thich Nhat Hanh writes, "To know that we are alive, that we can be in contact with all the wonders within us and around us, this is truly a miracle. We need only to open our eyes and to listen carefully to enjoy life's richness. In using conscious breathing, we can transform the present moment into a moment full of wonder and beauty."

Similar meditations in this style can be found in *The Blooming of a Lotus* by Thich Nhat Hanh. *The Miracle of Mindfulness* and *Peace Is Every Step*, by the same author, also explain more about this form of meditation.

Lovingkindness Meditation

The following practice, called lovingkindness meditation, is a simple way of cultivating the qualities of the heart. The meditation begins by bringing attention to yourself and sending yourself feelings of kindness and care. You send yourself a wish for your own well-being. In this meditation, you focus on certain phrases that help you connect with this feeling. You are not trying to force anything; you are simply inviting and cultivating care for yourself and others to be present.

Sometimes we are able to do this meditation and experience great openness to ourselves and others, while at other times it seems like nothing is happening. Sometimes when we are trying to send love to someone it can feel a little phony and "made up." It feels like we are just **157** repeating words that we do not feel. But our willingness and capacity to cultivate the qualities of the heart slowly grows over time. Indeed, sometimes when it seems "nothing" is happening, more is happening than we think.

In this practice, we are not trying to force the heart open. Sometimes our heart will be closed during this practice, but as Stephen Levine asks, "Can we keep our heart open to our heart being closed?" Can we treat ourselves with kindness even when we are feeling very closed and shut down? Can we open our heart to ourselves just as we are?

The practice is more about inviting lovingkindness to be present, making room for it, so we can meet our joy and pain with a big heart, with a heart that is able touch our joy and pain with understanding. But if you do this meditation and "nothing" happens, notice the tendency to think that you did it wrong or failed. Even lovingkindness meditation can be another way of thinking less about ourselves. We are simply inviting lovingkindness to be present, and it may take several tries for you to get a better sense of the practice. But there is nothing to force or make happen, simply a process to observe, explore, and enjoy.

We are also not so much wishing that a particular event happens to someone, like, "May you win the lottery" or "May you get a date with John." But it is more like, "May you be happy." If you win the lottery, may you be happy. If you *don't* win the lottery, may you be happy. If you get a date with John, may you be happy. If you *don't* get a date with John, may you be happy. Winning the lottery may bring happiness or it may not. Of course, we can wish basic health and well-being for someone like, "May you be of good health" and "May you be safe from danger," but the focus is more on a person's happiness than on particular events. That someone finds happiness is the underlying force.

You can do this practice during daily life as well. If you are on a debate team and one of your teammates gets up nervously to give her speech, try silently sending her loving-kindness and see what happens. See if you can support her nonverbally while she is giving her presentation. Then if you really want a challenge, try sending well wishes to those on the opposing team. See if you might find a place in your heart to wish them well. You can still want to win the debate, but to do so in a way that is caring and friendly.

Lovingkindness is nothing special. Everyone wishes to be happy. Everyone wants to be loved. In this meditation we simply acknowledge that and begin to invite lovingkind-ness to be more present in our life. There is no one who deep down does not wish to happy. They may have strange ways of going about finding that happiness and they may seem completely without heart, but deep down they wish for the same happiness that we do.

Some people hear of this meditation and think that this may be useful to use with someone they really hate in order to get beyond those feelings. It is not advisable in the beginning because it is just too hard for most of us. While it may at some point be useful, it is usually best to tread slowly. We first cultivate our love of the people for whom we already feel some warmth. We then direct it to someone we see but do not know so well. Later we begin to offer it to those with whom we have difficulty. Again, if we try to force love, our heart often closes in fear. We can, however, nurture it with those that we do love, and begin to build the base for being able to be open our hearts even to those whom we do not get along with so well. Start small, and trust it to grow naturally.

Just like previous meditations, take it at your own pace. Read the following meditation several times through before giving it a try. Trust yourself, and most importantly, enjoy.

Lovingkindness Meditation

Find a comfortable sitting position. Let your body take an upright but relaxed position. Then gently let your eyes close.

Let the breath come and go as it will. Allow the breath to be just as it is.

Next reflect on the quality of lovingkindness. What might it mean to live with an open heart, with a heart that is light and free? What is this quality known as lovingkindness? Take a few moments to reflect on this quality.

Let arise in your mind an image of yourself. Maybe it is an image of how you look now, or maybe an image arises of you when you were younger. Simply notice whatever image of yourself arises.

Begin to direct toward yourself feelings of lovingkindness and care. Relate to yourself as if you were your only child. Say to yourself, "May I be happy. May I dwell in my heart. May I be free from suffering. May I be at peace."

Softly repeat these sayings to yourself, speaking from your heart to yourself. Send yourself wishes for your own happiness. Life can be so hard some times. We all have endured so much. Gently begin to open your heart to yourself, to this being you are who wishes so much to be happy.

Repeat the phrases, "May I be happy. May I dwell in my heart. May I be free from suffering. May I be at peace." Gently opening your heart to yourself. Touching your own goodness, your longing to be happy.

"May I be happy. May I dwell in my heart. May I be free from suffering. May I be at peace." Repeating the words that bring healing. Making room in your heart for yourself. Softening. Allowing the love in. Letting yourself receive your own care.

Next bring to mind someone for whom you have much love. Maybe a close friend or an important mentor or someone who has shown you some kindness and care. Let the image, the feeling of them, arise in your mind. Then gently offer your lovingkindness to them. Repeating softly, "May you be happy. May you dwell in your heart. May you be free from suffering. May you be at peace."

Gently open your heart to this being who has shown you kindness. Let your heart open to them. Wish them well. Know that just as you wish to be happy, so too do they. Allow your heart to open to this other being.

Repeating softly in your heart, "May you be happy. May you dwell in your heart. May you be free from suffering. May you be at peace."

No force, just allowing the love that is there to be expressed, to be shared. Gently sending this person feelings of lovingkindness. Letting your heart touch theirs. Opening your heart to whatever degree the moment allows.

Continue to repeat softly, "May you be happy. May you dwell in your heart. May you be free from suffering. May you be at peace."

Then let the image of them fade. Let them go on their way.

Next bring to mind someone you do not know. Someone you see but maybe have spoken to very little or not at all. Maybe it is the person who drives the bus, the cashier at the local store, or a person in a class. Let the image, the feeling of them arise.

Begin to gently send them feelings of lovingkindness. Send them your wish for their well-being. Realizing that even though you do not know them, their heart is as yours. They too wish to be free of suffering. They too wish to be happy.

Repeat softly in your heart, "May you be happy. May you dwell in your heart. May you be free from suffering. May you be at peace."

Open your heart to this other being to whatever degree the moment allows. No force, simply invite lovingkindness to be present.

"May you be happy. May you dwell in your heart. May you be free from suffering. May you be at peace."

Opening, allowing, letting your heart touch theirs. Send them the depth of your lovingkindness and care. Offer lovingkindness to this being that you do not know so well. Gently repeat in your heart, "May you be happy. May you dwell in your heart. May you be free from suffering. May you be at peace."

Then allow this lovingkindness to spread through the room in which you sit. Send it to everyone in the house or the area surrounding you. Expand it to everyone in the town or area in which you live. Touch all the plants and animals with lovingkindness. Wish all beings well.

Expand this awareness to include the entire country. Wish all beings in this country well. Whether they live in the south or east, the north or west. Then gently expand to include all the continents. Africa, Asia, North America, Europe, South America, Australia. Sending your lovingkindness to all beings, no matter their skin color or belief system. To the young and old, the learned and unlearned. Touch all beings with lovingkindness. Expand this to including all the oceans. All the animals and plant life that exist in the ocean.

Expand this lovingkindness further until the whole world is embraced by it. The whole world becomes like a bubble floating in your heart.

Say softly in your heart, "May all beings be happy. May all beings dwell in their heart. May all beings be free from suffering. May all beings be at peace."

Wish all beings well.

"May all beings be happy. May all beings dwell in their heart. May all beings be free from suffering. May all beings be at peace."

For more information on this type of meditation, please consult Sharon Salzberg's *Lovingkindness: The Revolutionary Art of Happiness*.

Part Four

Finding Balance

Find Your Middle Way

Finding our way in life takes courage and exploration. The Buddha spoke of finding the "middle way," and his life can be seen as a search for that. He was raised in a palace full of every luxury imaginable. His parents tried to hide all suffering from him, and he was only allowed to leave the palace at certain times. They controlled what parts of the city he could visit so that he would not come in touch with suffering. He lived a very sheltered life, full of the greatest pleasures but lacking in meaning.

One day he sneaked out of the palace with his charioteer and went to a part of the city he had never seen. There he saw life in a new way: He saw an old person, a sick person, and a dead person. He asked his charioteer what was wrong with these people, and his charioteer explained that this happens to everyone, that everyone grows old, gets sick, and dies. The Buddha, known as Siddhartha at this time, was shocked. He never knew that suffering existed and that all people were subject to the laws of nature. While on this trip he also saw a monk who had renounced the world in search of the ultimate truth. He then decided that he too would seek the ultimate truth and find a way to live happily in a world of sickness, old age, and death. This became his quest.

He shaved his head and left his palace to live homeless in the forest. There he met a group of people who were practicing very intensively. They viewed the world of the senses—hearing, smelling, tasting, touching, seeing—as the problem in life. They wanted to deprive themselves of foods and any sensory input in the hopes of finding freedom. The Buddha followed their ways very strictly and even went for some time eating only one grain of rice a day. The goal was to deny most bodily wishes and shut out all sense doors in the hopes of experiencing freedom. While he experienced various levels of concentration, he did not find the peace he had hoped for. One day, when he was about to die of hunger, he realized the uselessness of his strategy. He realized that there was nothing inherently wrong in the senses. He saw that finding peace was not about trying to satisfy every desire, nor was it about denying his body and mind, but that there was a middle way between the two. Previously, he had lived in luxury where every one of his desires was met, but he was still unhappy. Now he realized that trying to deny the body and the senses did not lead him to peace either. He sought a way where he was not at the mercy of the senses nor in denial of them. Thus, the Buddha found the middle way between these two extremes.

The two stages the Buddha went through can be found in other ancient myths as well. However, most of us have gone through them in our own way. At times we thought that getting all we can from life, satisfying every desire without limit, was the answer to freedom. Other times we tried to push away the world, and thought that if we could run far enough away from it, we could find peace. Both these strategies take much effort and leave us tired from either chasing or running away. Most of us need to take one road as far as we can before we realize that we need to turn around. Then we see that neither indulging nor denying seems to work, and that we each must find our middle way of walking in the world.

For me, I remember wanting to be an oil man when I was younger. My friend's father was in the oil business and they had all the best stuff—a swimming pool, fancy cars, and lots of money to play. I thought, *This is the good life.*

They were able to satisfy many of their desires. My friend had nice clothes, the coolest games, and the best and biggest room of all my friends. Naturally I wanted what they had, and thought if I became an oil man, I would get it. Sign me up.

However, I later realized that though their money brought them some pleasure, it also brought them unhappiness. They still argued over money, and complained that they could not afford certain luxuries that their wealthier friends could afford. There were lawsuits and fights over money between relatives. Strangely enough, they did not think they had enough money, either. I began to see that while money was nice to have, it did not solve the problems of life.

I later went through a time as a complete loner, where I never went out with the few friends I had or enjoyed myself at all. All my desires were denied, since I figured nothing matters anyway. I thought, *I don't want to have any fun because there is no use in it.* I went through three or four years of complete isolation. I never dated or went to parties, but secretly hoped for more joy and happiness in my life.

I still feel like I am finding that middle way, and I see that there is a difference between what brings true joy and what just satisfies a desire. The middle way tells us that

169

there is a way to embrace life without becoming lost and overwhelmed. The middle way is the way of harmony, of effort without struggle.

Try This

Your Search for the Middle Way

Reflect on your own search to find a middle way. What stages have you been through so far? What stage do you feel like you are in? It may be helpful to write down your life story up until now. One time I spent five months at my father's house writing down my life story, what I could remember of it, that is. I had thought that it would be a book that I published, but when I finished I realized that I needed to write this material down for myself, not for others. I needed to do it as a way of "catching up with myself."

What have you tried and what have you learned so far? What are your current goals and priorities? Life is a learning process, and it can be helpful to not just look ahead, but to also reflect on where we have been so far. Take the time to reflect on your life and see if you too have been searching for a "middle way."

Images of Beauty

Images of beauty are offered to us everywhere. We cannot help but be influenced by the images of beauty we receive from magazines, movies, and other places. These images of beauty do, however, change. For many years women were considered beautiful who were strong and robust. Currently there is a great emphasis on thinness. Who knows what it will be next?

The messages are at times contradictory. One must look sexy yet tough, smart yet innocent, fun-loving yet serious. You might feel like screaming back at society, "Make up your stupid mind!" These images of beauty can at times create a type of prison for us. We want to look like the images we see, we want to be considered beautiful, **171** but the task can seem too much. And often the task is almost impossible.

We often forget that incredible amounts of work go into the pictures we see of beautiful people in ads. There are makeup artists involved, special lighting, expensive clothes, and often several days of photo shots which are frequently downloaded and "touched up" on the computer, to create the image we see. It's not that the person is not beautiful; it's just that an enormous amount of work goes into creating the final image we see. Few of us have such help.

I don't mean to knock fashion. Well, not completely. Our style of dress is one of the ways we get to express ourselves—our tastes, our style, our interests. It's great to look nice and I look at fashion magazines sometimes. It's cool to see all the different styles designers come up with and buying the latest styles can be fun. But the difficulty comes when we take these images for real and believe that beauty only exists in one certain look (a look that we must copy exactly). When we do this, a constriction comes over us. It's like trying to fit into a jacket that is a few sizes too small.

I grew up as a tall, awkward, skinny guy in a part of the country where big was in, at least for men. I went through a time of hating my body, wishing I had muscles, a bigger build, and a stronger presence. Most of my dislike of myself was felt in my belly, which was often tight and painful. I drank a lot of dairy products to try to soothe some of the discomfort I felt, but it only helped momentarily. Interestingly, meditation was one of the tools that helped me. When I began to soften the muscles of my belly and send feelings of acceptance toward my body, the discomfort began to lessen. It did not happen all at once, but I realized that my body craved an attention that was kind and accepting—and that for several years I'd been sending it just the opposite. Strangely, once I was able to do this, my appearance seemed to change as well and I became a little more outgoing and confident. It was not like everything was perfect, but the pain in my stomach and the hatred I felt towards my body lessened, which was a great relief.

I don't think the real issue is looking or not looking beautiful; it is more our attitude about ourselves. We can look our best as a means of self-respect and dignity, or we can try to look good because deep down we think we are worthless or do so to try to "show up" someone else. We can also not care for our body and let ourselves fall apart because we lack self-respect. Self-respect seems to be key.

However, we get so much conditioning in our society that beauty is synonymous with self-respect, and it is simply not true. I recently heard a radio commercial advertising face lifts, which said something like, "Find the face you've always been looking for. Go to FabulousFacelifts.com and find real beauty." No joke. Some people might really need face lifts, especially those unfortunate enough to be in car wrecks or other accidents that cause facial damage, but do the rest of us really need plastic surgery? If we do this, will we have the self-respect and self-confidence we so desire? I'm not so sure. Of course we want to be beautiful, but there is a natural beauty that comes from living a rich and meaningful life that is so much more beautiful than anything surgery can do. And it costs a lot less. Our country spends millions of dollars a year on plastic surgery while so many kids go without adequate food and clothing. It's crazy.

We are influenced by images of beauty on so many subtle levels. Our eyes glance at the cover of a magazine with a very attractive person on the cover. Instantly we think, "Man, I've got to get in shape," or "I should have bigger breasts," or "I need to start taking steroids." Of course, we do not always act on such thoughts but they still affect us. These images of beauty are, however, culturally influenced. In poor countries, for example, weight is often a sign of success for women. It means that you came from a wealthy family who could afford good food. If you are thin, then you must have come from a poor family who could not afford luxuries. People *try* to gain weight.

I am not arguing that weight should be a sign of success or failure, but that our beliefs are in large part affected by the society. If we are thin in the United States, we mainly get messages of approval. If we are thin in the poor country of Bangladesh, people look at us as if we are poor and lack the means to buy food. We have not changed at all, just the culture has. Thinness is thinness and heaviness is heaviness. Anything added on top of that is extra. There is no inherent good or bad in either. The dance, I think, is learning to take of ourselves—exercising, wearing clothes we like, eating healthy foods—but not getting so carried away by it that we lose perspective and think that our body must look one particular way. In our society today, this is not an easy dance to do.

Strangely, even the people who *do* fit the traditional images of beauty often have low self-esteem. *I'm not beautiful; my nose is too big; my ears are too small; my lips are not right; you should see me without makeup.* There is always something. Sometimes it seems like we lose no matter what. How on earth do we survive? Rather than try to fit into one image of beauty, maybe we need a larger definition of beauty. Maybe beauty can have a big nose or large head, or whatever. Maybe our beauty can spring from within us. Maybe there is a way to live beauty rather than continually striving for it in one single image. Just an idea.

To Practice or Not to Practice, This Is Not the Question

There is much talk of practice—meditation practice, spiritual practice, etc. One might think, *Practice, practice, practice—when is the performance? If it's all a practice, when do I get a break? Can I call a time-out?*

Others may ask, *If I practice, am I a better person? If I don't, am I less of a person?* What does it actually mean to practice? Can we not practice? In a way all this talk about practice can be misleading. Not practicing is kind of like not living. Can you not live? You can kill yourself, but that may only change the nature of life. You don't know, but possibly you soon experience another birth or part of your consciousness continues in some other form. Who knows? Maybe even death does not end life.

There seems to be a general desire in each of us to awaken, to experience greater freedom and wisdom. I don't know where it comes from, but it seems to exist in everyone. There is a desire to be happy, to live this life the best we can. In this sense, we are always looking for ways to gain richness and aliveness; we are always looking for ways to live more fully. When we meet someone who is kind and wise, we naturally want to be around them. Initially, we may not know why, but we are drawn by some desire for happiness. In this sense, can we ever not practice? Can we ever give up that move toward greater happiness and freedom? We may be able to push it away for a short time, but I don't think we can ever get rid of it. A practice to me is simply activities that help us follow this calling for self-knowledge and greater understanding. On one level, all life is a practice. In this sense, to practice or not to practice, this is not the question. The question is: How can we further cultivate the qualities of the heart that help us live a richer life? Anything that helps ease some of the pain and suffering in this crazy world and brings us more joy is a blessing. Anything that helps us find more care for ourselves and others is a rare and precious jewel.

However, it is easy to lose sight of this movement toward wisdom and compassion and get caught in the whirlwind of life, where we feel thrown back and forth aimlessly. The practice, then, is remembering our greater purpose, and following the calling of our heart for more peace and freedom. Bo Lozoff writes, "The great problem of the world is that human life, the human journey, is very deep, while the modern mainstream culture is not." Each of us is deep and caring, and we can easily forget this and focus on less important goals, goals that do not value the depth of our true nature. Creating a life that supports this greater calling is a practice. It takes effort to let go of the temptations that pull us away from that calling and to stay with what truly satisfies us.

As always, easier said than done. No kidding. But luckily there are many traditions and practices to remind us of what is important to us and lead us back. We are not better people if we practice something like meditation or anything else, but in this journey we might as well use all the tools we can.

To practice or not to practice, this is not the question. The question is how can we live fully, how can we live and be the deep, caring people that we are?

Somebodyness and Our True Nature

Everyone wants to feel comfortable with themselves. Everyone wants to feel loved and accepted. When we do not feel this way, when our sense of who we are is not strong, we act in various ways to try to make up for our lack of self-worth. Some people try to feel good about themselves by putting others down. Others seem to need everyone's attention in order to feel adequate. When our self-worth is not strong, we often manipulate ourselves to get validation from the outside world.

When we have a low sense of ourselves, we often try to be "somebody." We put an image out to the world that we are a particular kind of person—a cool person, a with-it person, whatever. We build up an outer image that is often **179** very different from how we feel inside. Inside we may feel very hollow and lonely, but outwardly we try to show that we are something else. We could call this quality of trying to make the world see us in only one particular way our "somebodyness." Our somebodyness is the image we put out to others; it is the degree to which we mold ourselves in situations so that people will only see what we want them to see.

In Zen Buddhism they talk about our "original" or "true" nature. This is not so much something we become; it is something we already are. This nature is beyond images or ideas. It is not something we gather or obtain, but is more something we see and allow. The Buddha talked about the unborn or the deathless. This is the greatness of our true nature that was never born and never dies. Talking about this state does little; it can only be experienced and touched. The difference between our somebodyness and our true nature is that true nature does not rely on the admiration and praise of others. In this place we do not need to put others down in order to feel whole. It is not based on an I'm-better-than-you or an I'm-less-than-you position, but is the freedom to be who we are in any given moment. As Lao-tzu put it: "When you are content to simply be yourself and don't compare or compete, everybody will respect you."

Often we think that to feel good about ourselves, we must feel a bit above others—wiser, stronger, or more talented. We think only the people at the top of the class deserve to feel good about themselves since they have reason to. One's true nature, however, does not need a reason to blossom. It is not dependent on being at the top or the bottom of the class. It is something else. It is a non-comparing state where we see that we are not much different than others. Though we think of ourselves as one type of person and someone else as another type of person, it is not so easy to separate the two. Once this separation weakens, there is less of a need to compare and build up one's image in comparison to others.

This does not mean that we all act or dress the same way. We still have our personality and our unique expression of this true nature. Our true nature can be cool or hip, but there is not the comparison and struggle behind it. You can dress like a fashion model, or gothic, or grunge. It is not so much determined by dress, but more by attitude, an attitude that is not putting others down or pretending to be a certain way. Our true nature is not so much expressed in one particular way, but rather it comes from our heart, from our aliveness, and not from fear or struggle. It is like the blossoming of a flower. The flower wants to blossom; it wants to show itself. We simply need to give it the adequate conditions. We need to trust and make room for it.

If someone asks you, "Who are you?" you might answer that you are a young man or young woman, student or teacher, skateboarder or jock. While all these answers may be true, none of these can describe the vastness of your true nature. Even answering "I am a spiritual person" is limiting because it is based on our ideas of what a spiritual person is. None of these labels are absolute, unchanging truths. Some people will answer, "I am an intelligent person." If we identify ourselves as an intelligent person, then who are we when we get Alzheimer's later in life or become somewhat senile and cannot even remember what we had for breakfast? Or who are we when we get brain disease or when our mind simply does not work so well? Who are we when we no longer fit the label we have for ourselves?

Of course, in conversation we need to use words to describe the different roles we play in life. In a particular situation, we are a student or band member or sister. But when it comes down to describing our true nature, words do not do it. Our roles in life as a student, athlete, or cheerleader, all have a relative truth, but we are much more than these roles. There is something more than all this that cannot be described, but it can be experienced. It shines when we let out the truth of our experience, when we do not hold back the full expression of our being. There is no way we can control or manipulate it. We can only open to it and allow it to come through by a kind of inner trust.

Just Say OM!

I once visited a renowned Burmese meditation master to get his signature on a VISA application so I could go study with him in Burma, a country in Southeast Asia, which has been renamed Myanmar by the military government. When I met him, he asked through a translator why I practiced meditation. I answered that I wanted to better know my mind so as to suffer less and to create less suffering in the world. I thought that was a fairly good answer. He surprised me by responding, "Don't you want the ultimate bliss?" *The ultimate bliss*, I thought. It sounded oddly similar to what kids said to me in the park after school when offering me a joint. I checked with the translator to make sure I had heard right. Yep, he said the ultimate bliss. The "bliss" talked **183** about in spiritual traditions and the "high" of drugs have interesting parallels.

Some years ago during the Reagan administration, the government created a program focused on young people and drugs called, "Just Say No." They asked teens to just say no to drugs. While this can be useful and may be the best strategy for some, just saying no without saying yes to something else can simply lead to other addictions. Someone says no to drugs, but they just change their addiction from illegal drugs to cigarettes, to alcohol, to shopping, to caffeine, or a million other things. While certain addictions are less damaging than others, the issue is not so simple.

We all seek calm, peace, and wisdom. We seek states of mind and body that give us a clearer picture of ourselves. Many people who take drugs are longing for altered states that give them a glimpse of freedom. Many of the young people I work with say that drugs help their body to relax and their mind to stop worrying. It is similar to experiences people have with meditation and other spiritual practices. We then explore more direct and less harmful ways to touch that same place of calm and ease. For some people, the exploration does not end with just saying no, but with saying yes to something that truly fulfills this greater longing. This might be found in music or theater or sports or meditation or a combination of all of these.

Anytime someone talks openly about drugs there is often a great deal of fear in the room. Parents claim that they never tried drugs, or if they did, their kids should definitely not. It's a hard topic for parents and elders to explore because they fear saying something that will somehow encourage a young person to become addicted. *You can't talk about drugs,* some claim. *It is better if it is never mentioned.* I certainly do not recommend them, but for any understanding, we need open communication. We need to hear both sides of an issue. As long as topics remain locked up in the closet, understanding is not possible.

When I was younger my brother often shielded drugs from me so I did very little experimentation in my teens. My brother, two and a half years my elder, was trying everything that came down the pike during his teen years. While he was experimenting, he was continually making sure I never started. He would say, "Believe me, it is better if you never begin." He got angry at his friends if they tried to include me in their experimentations. I believed him, for the most part, and drugs never became a big part of my life.

I think communication is important. There are families where drugs are labeled as evil, and the children, unable to speak openly about their desires and concerns, often begin taking everything imaginable, often in very damaging ways, once they move out of the house and can make their own decisions. Had they been able to speak openly about drugs with their parents, they may have been able to find a better balance. Communication seems to be essential.

Drugs, however, can certainly be damaging. Talk with any addict, and they will tell you about the pain and misery of addiction, about what it is like to live for that next hit. Many crimes today are committed to get money to feed a heroin or cocaine addiction. Seventy percent of those in prison are there for drug-related crimes. Babies are born addicted to heroin or cocaine and live in great pain and misery because of this. Much of the child abuse and spousal abuse committed in our country today is by people who are under the influence of alcohol. Alcohol is also the source of many health problems. The personal health and social detriment caused by drug abuse is immense.

In certain spiritual teachings, they chant the word "OM." They say that this is the great sound of the universe. Whatever we do, we are seeking spiritual connection. So rather than just say no, maybe we need to "Just Say OM." Maybe we need to find ways to enrich our spiritual life. After many years of exploration with drugs, the author and spiritual teacher Ram Dass said of drugs, "They could get me high, but they couldn't get me free." No matter what we decide to do or not do or try or not try, it is this greater freedom that we seek.

Warning: Change Ahead

If someone were to ask you what is one thing that you know for sure, what would you say? You may possibly answer that everything changes. You may not know what will happen in the future, but you can be sure of one thing: it will be different than it is now. Everything changes—beliefs, bodies, parents, friends. The wealthiest person in the world cannot stop it, and the greatest armies are at its mercy. Change is the great force that cannot be stopped, but you can learn to make friends with it.

Some people think that since everything changes, why try or why care about anything? *Life is going to end sooner or later, so what difference does it make what I do? Everything dies, so nothing matters. Whether I act cruelly or kindly makes no difference, since everything changes anyhow. The hungry person will eventually get food. They don't need my help. I don't care. It doesn't matter.*

This is not a harmonious relationship with change. This is a giving in to the force of change, a closing of one's eyes to life, a lack of participation. This uses the truth of change as a justification for not living. This says since people die, why love them? It's a guarding of the heart, a wish to not let the heart open for fear it will break. It does not realize that a life with no love is much more painful than a life of participation and care, that an aching heart is better than no heart.

Another strategy is to try and make our life a certain way, then attempt to stop change. We think if we can create the perfect conditions, then stop life, we will find peace. *If I can just get the perfect mate, the perfect job, the perfect friends, then I will be able to relax.* But even if one is able to create such conditions, they do not last. If we attach ourselves to the conditions of life rather than our response to life, having everything go our way can be terribly frightening. We fear losing those conditions and try frantically to hold on to what by its nature cannot be held on to. The moment of greatest praise from the world can be the scariest because we worry about how to sustain that praise and realize how far down the pedestal we can fall.

When at the top, the distance down is the greatest. Setting and reaching goals is wonderful, but there is no way to freeze life at a particular time and think that change can be subdued.

The truth is that every moment is a moment of change. Our body is not what it was yesterday, nor are our parents, nor are our friends. Though many of us only realize the truth of change in those "big moments," change is occurring all the time. No thought stays very long, body sensations continue to arise and pass away. Even if we try to hold on to a particular thought, we can't. The greatest thought does not stay, nor does the worst pain. While this may seem like life dealt us a bad deal, there is something comforting in change. Change is what allows for children to grow up, for ourselves to develop and mature, for gardens to blossom. As much as we hate change at times, it is also the greatest of friends at other moments. While in pleasant moments we may wish for change to never come, in moments of pain, it is what we pray for.

Change shows us clearly that we are not in complete control of what happens in life. The mind has all kinds of ideas about what will happen in the future, but it is not always right. Though there can be some use in planning and predicting, the truth is that we do not know what may occur. When we forget the mystery of life, change becomes the enemy we try to capture. It is the force we fight against to make sure everything goes the way we want. This is a losing battle since, in the end, change always wins out.

So how do we relate to change? How do we love and live knowing that everything passes? What is it all about? I wish there was a one-word answer, but I think it is a personal process. Each of us is asked to explore our relationship to change. Neither denying change nor trying to stop change seems to work. Rather than fight or give in to change, the question then becomes how can change be an ally? How can the truth of change be a reminder to relish each moment and not postpone life?

Since change is the only constant, it can also be the best reminder. It can remind us that there is no time to hold back. Since we do not know what will happen in the future, we might as well live and love now. There is no better time. There is no better time to tell our friends, parents, and loved ones that we care about them, no better time to let out the full expression of our heart, no better time to give someone a gift or do a kind act.

It is easy to get overwhelmed by change. We turn twenty and think that we have wasted our entire life. There is no hope for us. We have not proved ourselves yet and never will. It is all over. Nothing will ever change. Some people turn twenty, and completely give up on life, thinking that they have already missed all possible opportunities. They have the spirit of what you would think an eighty-year-old might have. Other people are eighty years old, but have the spirit of an optimistic twenty-year-old. Their body may be old, but they have a youthful, vibrant spirit.

Whether we like it or not, change is a companion for life. It is a sometimes wonderful and sometimes painful companion, but there is no getting rid of it. The mystery may not get any clearer as we mature, but our wonder can grow so that the truth of change becomes an ally. While we cannot subdue it, we can learn from it that life need not be postponed.

You Own More Than You Think

On one level, we own nothing. Everything belongs to the earth, which belongs to the universe, which belongs to . . . On another level, we own everything, we are one with everything. The ocean is ours, as is the sky, as are the trees. They are a part of this web to which we belong.

We can also look at ownership in terms of gratefulness. The Benedictine monk Brother David Steindl-Rast talks about the importance of gratefulness in spiritual practice. He says that this gratefulness springs from a sense of belonging. We can only feel connected with something that we appreciate. Another way to view ownership is to look at what we have that we are grateful for and with which we feel a sense of belonging.

There may be a beautiful garden in your neighbor's yard. Your neighbor hires a gardener to take care of it, but he only glances at the garden when he goes by it on his way to and from work. He does not really see or appreciate it. Though the garden is officially his, the gardener who works on it and the neighbors who come by and look at it get more joy from the garden than he does. They see the changes in the garden during each season, smell the flowers, and it brings them great joy.

So who really owns the garden? We could say that we only own that which we can appreciate. This ownership does not mean that others do not also own it, but that what we can appreciate connects us to our sense of belonging, and in this way we are nurtured by it. So whose name is on the official papers really matters little. Some of the wealthiest people in the world can actually "own" very little in the true sense. There is very little they feel grateful for. We can own huge amounts of land and other objects, but without gratefulness, our sense of belonging is not nurtured. They are officially "ours" but they give us little true nourishment or joy. However, when we see with acceptance and appreciation, that which we see becomes a part of us, belongs to us. Lao-tzu writes, "When you realize there is nothing lacking, the whole world belongs to you."

Thich Nhat Hanh has said, "Our actions are our only true belongings." The life we live, the degree to which we cultivate awareness and compassion, is the true sign of our life. Our true belongings are much more than the clothes we have in our closet or the car we drive or the size of the house we live in. Our true belongings, our true ownership, is more than any amount of money can buy. It is our ability to live in alignment with our heart.

Find True Friends

Finding true friends is no easy task. It takes work, and usually some heartache. Some people think that they can live without friends, but I certainly cannot. Friends help give us support in times of difficulty and help celebrate the many successes and joys that come our way.

It is easy to give up on friends because of the difficulty they can sometimes cause. We might be spending time with someone who we think is our friend, and later learn that she no longer wants to spend time with us, is dating the guy we recently broke up with, or told lies about us behind our back. We wonder how someone can be so cruel. There have been people in my life who I thought I was getting to be friends with, only to later have them completely ignore me. It hurts, but I'm certain that I've behaved the same way to others.

It's amazing how close we can feel to another person. Sometimes we can feel so close that it's scary. This is both the great quality of friendship and also what makes it hurt so much when the friendship does not work out. We feel so close that when one of us does something to hurt the other, it cuts right to the heart.

But this does not mean that friends are worthless or that all friends will someday hurt us. It simply means that most friendships take some work. We may meet someone and after a week or so think that we really know them, but it usually takes more time. People are too complex to get to know in a short amount of time.

Friends need not just be people who enjoy the same activities that we do—who listen to the same music, work at the same job, wear the same clothes, etc. Friendship is about a mutual care and concern for each other's well-being. A friend is someone we trust and who encourages us to live our dreams—someone who listens more than advises, who understands and does not judge. They need not be the wisest or most intelligent person on earth, but they do need to hear us, and to try to see from our viewpoint.

There are people who just want to hang out with us because we are popular or they want something from us, but they are not true friends. They will not be around if we lose our popularity. Their attention is simply based on certain conditions, and when those conditions change, they are gone. There are also groups of people or cliques who consider themselves friends, but they do not really know one another at all. They don't share hopes and dreams. It is mainly about outer appearances and being in the "in group." These "friendships" tend not to last that long.

If we think ahead twenty to thirty years and think about what kind of friends we would want, it gives a bigger perspective. You have graduated from school, maybe gotten married, have a few kids and a regular job, etc. You have been through hard times and very happy times. What kind of person will you want to be your friend through all of this? What qualities would you like them to possess?

Friendships should increase, not decrease, the respect we give others. There are certain groups of "friends" who treat most people outside their group with criticism and ridicule. This just makes our world smaller. Our friends should help broaden our sense of friendliness, not limit it. They should help us relate respectfully to more and more people. They should help make our world bigger.

Too many friendships come and go like the wind. Even just one good friend in this life is such a blessing. One person whom we can count on and tell our fears and hopes to can make all the difference in the world.

Qualities of a Friend

Reflect on what qualities are most important to you in a friendship. Make a list of the qualities that you think are essential for a genuine relationship. Write down as long a list as you can. Reflect on the friendships in your life and see whether these qualities have been present. If so, how did they show themselves? What helped them be present in the relationship? If not, how can you bring these qualities into your current and future friendships? What does this list say about the kind of friends you want?

Community

We have a great tradition of individualism in the United States that says, "I don't need anyone. I can do it myself." The lone ranger heading out to do battle alone. While this attitude can be useful at times, at other times it can block our growth. Everyone needs help at times; we need our friends, family, and community.

Even if you could tackle all the problems of life on your own, would you want to? Much of the joy is in sharing the process with others. If you reflect on your highest moments, I'm guessing that many of these moments were shared with others—winning the championship basketball game, or performing in a successful play, or going on a weekend trip with friends. Even if you are involved in an individual sport **199** like tennis, you could not do well without your coach, your family, and your friends. No person succeeds without a great deal of help from others.

When we see that our learning has rarely occurred alone, we know the importance of a supportive community. Community reminds us that life is not about a race to get ahead of everyone else, but a way of being with others that supports a feeling of togetherness and mutual support. None of us are problem-free all the time. The more supportive friends and guides we have in our life, the more help we can give and receive.

The desire to belong and feel loved and accepted is a deep longing. When I was younger, I remember going with my father to pick out a jacket for the winter. All the popular kids at my school wore these expensive jackets with the brand name "Members Only" on the front. The jackets were thin, and not very durable. They were overpriced and inadequate for a winter jacket, but I wanted one just for the name. I thought wearing the right jacket would make me a part of the "in" group.

I got the jacket but did not feel the sense of belonging that I had hoped for. Soon styles changed, and there was a new brand that I had to get to stay "in the club." The satisfaction I had hoped for in purchasing the jacket never came. I had thought that jacket would satisfy my desire to belong. It did not. It was one of the first times I remember feeling this great desire to belong, and wanting to find some way to satisfy it.

But we can never find a sense of belonging in being a part of a particular group or in wearing the right clothes. Our sense of belonging must come from a greater sense of community, one that does not require us to hang out with certain people or to purchase particular objects. It is a way of being, of seeing the world. It includes our relationship to all life, including the trees, animals, insects, and every living being.

You can take on a practice like meditation and actually use it as a way of becoming more isolated and withdrawn. While this may be a cycle you need to go through, eventually the practice asks you to engage with the larger community. You may begin to think that only meditation is important, and that all other people are simply "distractions." I don't think this is the best view to take. Any insight or awakening you experience through a practice like meditation needs to find a way to be shared within the larger community. Unless you are planning to live alone in a cave for the rest of your life, eventually you must find a way to live with and support the community around you.

For a sense of community, I think that it helps to have contact with people from a variety of age groups. We need time with our peers, but we also need time with elders and with kids. Spending time with elders, we see the value of life experience and get a chance to hear stories of times past. Spending time with younger people, we are reminded of the changes we've been through and we see the need to guide the next generation. By having contact with a variety of age groups, we can see ourselves, as we were and as we will be. This is invaluable wisdom.

Elders-in-Training

Billions of people have lived before us, making both horrendous mistakes and discovering enormous insights. Some of this hard-earned wisdom has been passed down and is available to us, but we must first be open to learning it. In India, there is a saying, "When a pickpocket meets a saint, all he sees are the saint's pockets." If we are not open to learning, the most brilliant person could be right in front of us, and we will not notice.

So it takes a certain openness to learn. When I hitchhiked in my early twenties, I got picked up by all kinds of people. Sometimes I would find myself on a long cross-country ride with a farmer from Idaho. I would often sit there somewhat bored, thinking that he and I had absolutely nothing in common. I was a hard core environmentalist, what did I have to learn from an Idaho farmer who made his living off the land? Duh. Then one day I realized that everyone had wisdom to share if only I knew the right questions to ask. I could sit in the car bored for five hours or I could use it as an opportunity to learn. I realized that this farmer sitting next to me had unique stories and knowledge that I might never get a chance to learn from again—about growing crops, living on a farm, tending animals, and much more.

So I began asking people questions, finding out about all their struggles and joys, successes and failures. I learned through this that everyone has wisdom to share if someone asks them the right questions. And people *want* to share their wisdom. With no one to pass on hard-earned wisdom to, what use is it? There are many wise elders who want to pass on their stories and experiences, but they are not given the chance.

Some people think that elders in our culture are "behind the times." They do not understand what it is to be young, so who needs them? But this attitude is really our loss. Spiritual teachings have been passed down for generations from elders to youth, primarily by word of mouth. It has been this one-on-one contact where the deepest teachings have been shared. This is often lost in our high-tech world that focuses more on e-mails and faxes than on one-on-one contact.

I don't mean to imply that every old person is some kind of saint just because they are old. There are certainly some old people who are racist and judgmental and a pain to be around—agreed. But it is still valuable to make the effort to listen to their stories and bring out the wisdom they have to offer. I think one of the greatest sorrows in life is dying without feeling that you have contributed anything positive to society, feeling that what you have learned has not been passed on. It is important that people be given a chance to share their stories in hopes that someone may benefit from them.

We need the stories from the elders in our family and community, but we also need guidance from those in a particular spiritual tradition. If you follow a particular spiritual path, you need the help of elders in that tradition. It's not like you cannot learn on your own, but life is hard enough, so why not get all the help you can? The role of the elder is an important one, and it's a role that we will all likely someday occupy. We are all "elders-in-training."

Rely on Nature

People have always gone to nature to seek guidance. Whether it is through long walks, or vision quests in the woods or the desert, nature helps us more easily access a deeper kind of guidance. It allows us into the world where visions and guidance are born. Initiations for young people in a tribe or village have also primarily been conducted through intensive contact with the world of nature.

Spending time in nature is a wonderful way to help us gain clarity and vision. Nature invites and encourages us to be aware. The colors, the smells, the sight of a river or tree all awaken our senses and increase our awareness of life. When we are alone in the woods or at the edge of a river, a

sense of ease and calm often comes over us and our breath

tends to be fuller. This ease and calm is accessible in all moments of life, but nature makes it even more so.

Anyone who has spent time in nature knows that the natural world is not always pleasant and sweet. It can be fierce and rough. Strong winds, powerful rainstorms, snow storms, and the like demand our respect. Some plants are poisonous and some animals are dangerous. Nature shows us beauty while teaching us about the respect needed to enjoy that beauty.

Paying attention to nature helps us learn about cycles and change. Watching the flower in our front yard, we see that it has a time when only the stalk is visible, and a time when the flower blooms in all her beauty. We learn to see cycles and the process of change.

Nature also teaches us about silence. Most of our daily lives are filled with noise—of cars, music, televisions, and radios. Even when we sit by ourselves at home and are "doing nothing" there may be the sounds of the refrigerator, the computer, traffic outside, or the telephone. There are also sounds in nature, of trees swaying in the breeze or birds chirping, but these sounds have a more soothing quality to them. They tend to foster more ease and well-being.

If we go deeply enough into nature, we can touch the underlying silence that is there. Being around trees that are several hundred or even several thousand years old gives us a greater sense of history and belonging. When the Buddha gave his instructions for meditation practice he recommended going "to the forest, a foot of a tree, or an empty place." Many of the great spiritual teachers, when seeking guidance and nourishment, went off to the forest to connect themselves more fully with a spiritual force. Both the Buddha and Jesus went into nature to do intensive practice. Spending time in nature is great way to remember what is important and to touch that place of belonging in us all.

Nature is not as accessible as it was several thousand years ago when the Buddha and Jesus lived, but we can use and appreciate what we do have. Animals too can be great reminders of mindfulness and care. Some of the greatest teachers of what it is to love and forgive can be animals. Animals remind us that the longing for happiness is felt in more than just humans. All beings want to live without suffering. All living beings need care and attention in order to grow.

The world offers numerous reminders to help us be more alive. The sky above us, the grass in our yard, or the birds that visit in the morning are all our fellow companions. The more we notice them, the more we will be enriched by their presence, and the more we will be motivated to act to nurture and support their well-being. The great environmentalist Aldo Leopold writes, "It is inconceivable to me that an ethical relation to the land can exist without love, respect and admiration for the land, and a high regard for its value." In order to respect something we must learn to see, touch, and appreciate it.

The Buddha said that the wise live without injuring nature, as the bee drinks honey without injuring the flower. This is not very easy today in our complex world where it seems so many acts can damage nature. But any spiritual practice must attempt to honor all life forms. As Chief Seattle warned, "Whatever befalls the earth befalls the sons and daughters of the earth. We did not weave the web of life. We are merely a strand in it. Whatever we do to the web, we do to ourselves."

Try This

Guidance from Nature

Find one place in nature that is near your home, where you can go to chill out and get guidance. This is a place where you can be still and can take a step back from the busyness of your life. It could be on a bench, in a park, near a river, or under a tree. I like to find places where I can sit and no one can see me. It helps for me to have that sense of privacy, but see what feels right to you.

This is your place to kick it, to hang out when you need some time by yourself. Find one place where you feel you can be by yourself and reflect on life. Make sure to visit this place when you need guidance.

Part Five

Connecting to the World

Judgment Always Comes Back to Ourselves

I've been told that someone once asked the Buddha whether it was possible to be critical and judgmental of other people and not treat oneself the same way. The Buddha responded, no. He said that if one is critical and judgmental of others, it is impossible not to treat oneself the same. He basically said that if someone is not patient with others' shortcomings, she will not be patient with her own. If someone judges the appearance of others, saying how someone is ugly or stupid, she will criticize herself in the same way. While at times it appears that people can be judgmental toward others, but seem completely satisfied with themselves, the Buddha said that this is not possible, that how we treat others is how we treat ourselves.

Many people put forth a certain image that they have everything together. They think they have got it all figured out and that difficulty will never come their way. They make good grades, are with a beautiful boyfriend or girlfriend, and come from a family with lots of money. They think that they possess some special quality that allows them to always be ahead of everyone else and, therefore, are somehow better than others. But you never know what is coming around the next corner. The Buddha said that fortune changes like the swish of a horse's tail. If we judge others and think ourselves better, we may quickly find, to our disappointment, that we have switched positions with them and now hold the position that we had once judged.

Some people seem to need to treat others harshly in order to feel good about themselves. But if we look deeply, beyond critical words and the roles they play, we see that criticism and judgment carry a momentum that eventually returns to the one directing it towards others. This criticism does not just disappear. If we are judgmental of someone who made a mistake, we will be judgmental of ourselves when we make a mistake.

But in the same way, compassion and tolerance have an equal momentum to them, and by practicing tolerance and understanding with others, we are learning to bring those same qualities to ourselves. When Jesus spoke of

213

treating one's neighbor as oneself, he was possibly touching on this same point—that as we respond to others, we respond to ourselves. While many people seem to find some satisfaction in criticizing others, we not only end up treating ourselves the same way, but if we pay attention we can feel the effects of that criticism in our own bodies. Notice how your body feels after judging and criticizing someone. It's not just that if we criticize others, we will criticize ourselves the same way, but in that moment we too experience that judgment.

There is, however, a difference between remorse and judgment. When a memory arises of treating a friend harshly or lying to someone to get our way, we feel remorse, a momentary sadness of realizing that our actions were unskillful or unkind. We all at times act unconsciously and without consideration for others. When such memories arise, our face grimaces at the memory, and we think, "Did I really say that?" Often we then try to edit the memory to come out differently, trying to play back a different tape. However, when this does not succeed we realize, "Oh no, I *did* say that. What was I thinking?"

This is remorse and we are quite fortunate such a quality exists. This helps us to refine our actions and to live a more authentic life. It does not mean that we are useless and unworthy or that we made some mistake beyond repair. It simply means that we are human, and that like all humans, we are in a learning process. Remorse is actually a good sign. It means that we are becoming more aware, that what was previously unconscious is coming into consciousness. We don't need to beat ourselves up about it, but it is good to learn from the experience so we are less apt to repeat it. Think of a world with no remorse, with no ability to learn from our unskillful actions. Remorse is painful at times, but it is a sign that our awareness is deepening.

You might think, "That is easy to say, but I have really screwed up. I mean, I have done things that are beyond repair." We have all screwed up, but there is a way of acknowledging the truth of any experience and using that truth to help guide the rest of our life. Some of the greatest saints were robbers or murderers early in their life. As they say in Zen, "The greater the struggle, the greater the enlightenment."

One way to look at actions is to use the words skillful and unskillful. Rather than use words like sinful or bad, we can say that a certain action was unskillful, meaning that it caused suffering. A skillful action, then, is one that helps ease suffering, one that is done with awareness and compassion. To say that something is unskillful simply means that it was not done with awareness and compassion, that it caused or supported suffering. It means that you have learning ahead of you. Join the crowd.

Simple Problems Have Simple Answers

To quote Madonna, "We live in a material world." Our age is maybe more materialistic than any in history. We tend to be defined by the job we have, the clothes we wear, and the car we drive. The belief that money can buy happiness seems to be getting more popular each year. In a June 1997 *Time* magazine poll, 33 percent of Generation Xers agreed with the statement, "The only meaningful measure of success is money." Money and material comfort certainly have their place in life, but are they the only measure of success?"

There is a place in us all that thinks "If only . . . " *If only I had that car or job, or if only I had done that, or if only I was with so-and-so.* We all have a certain amount of grief that we carry around with us every day. There is the grief of not having what we want. There is also the grief of getting what we wanted and it not giving us the satisfaction we had hoped for. Deep down, we long for satisfaction.

Too often life gets very complex, so complex that we lose focus on what is really important in life. We take on more and more responsibilities, more and more tasks, and our life gets overwhelming. It used to be that just older people did this, but now it seems to occur in all age groups. There becomes no time just to relax.

There is a story about an American businessman who went to visit a small fishing village in South America. One day he saw a fisherman coming into the dock late in the morning. He asked the fisherman how many fish he caught that day.

"About ten," the man replied. "Two are for my family and the rest I sell in the market to cover expenses."

"What are you going to do the rest of the day?" the businessman asked.

"I'm just going to relax," replied the fisherman. "Spend time with my family, hang out with my friends, maybe take a nap."

The businessman could not understand this. "Why don't you work more?" the man inquired. "If you worked more hours and caught a few more fish, you could use that

217

money to buy a bigger net, then you could catch even more fish."

"If I caught more fish, what then?"

"You could eventually retire."

"What would I do if I retired?" asked the fisherman.

"Well, you could spend time with your family and friends and just relax."

"What do you think I'm doing now?" the fisherman replied.

Simplicity does not mean that we give away all our possessions, but rather it asks, what do I need and what can I do without, what possessions do I own and what possessions own me? We simplify not because we have to, or because something bad will happen to us if we don't; we simplify to enrich our own life. Sometimes the challenge in life is in working toward owning a home or getting a piece of land or starting your own business. These are wonderful goals and probably much satisfaction will come in achieving them, but it does not mean that our inner life will automatically be peaceful. No matter how many goals we reach, the work of the heart still needs attention. If we cannot enjoy the flower in our front yard or the evening sunset, how can we expect to enjoy a house or owning land? Without an awareness and appreciation of life, no purchase can really satisfy us. It is not in getting or having particular things that is the problem, only in thinking that they will give us ultimate satisfaction.

Numerous spiritual traditions speak of the importance of simplicity. Lao-tzu writes, "To attain knowledge, add things everyday. To attain wisdom, remove things everyday." Thoreau said, "I make my life rich by making my wants few." Jesus said that it is easier for a camel to go through the eye of a needle than for a rich man to go to heaven.

But it is not so important what others have said, but rather what our heart says, and what we need at a particular time. Simplicity is always an individual choice, depending on what we need at that time. At times we may need more possessions to do the work we believe in, but we need not look to these possessions as the source of our happiness or we will be greatly disappointed when they someday leave us. If we do not lose them before, death takes it all away.

The struggle for much of the world is not about how to let go of possessions, but how to get adequate food, clothing, and shelter. Many people are struggling to get by, and a piece of bread for them goes a long way. If we are fortunate enough to have adequate food and shelter, the more we can simplify, the more resources will be available to others and the more time and money we will have to give to others. Living a lifestyle of great wealth while others starve is no sign of success. If success was only about wealth, then most of the great spiritual leaders and artists in our history would be failures.

Rather than being the person at the top, our deeper longing is to feel that we belong. This sense of belonging only comes when our life is in alignment with the values of our heart. When we live in a way that we believe in, our sense of comradeship with other people and other life forms deepens. We don't need to struggle for twenty years for this experience. It is always available, but it asks us to live in alignment with our values. The hardest part about seeing another's suffering is feeling that we are living in a way that supports it. Likewise, when we feel we are living in a way that helps to relieve that suffering, our heart may ache but it does not close in fear. Simplicity simply means that we honor our relationship to the web of life.

Try This

A Reflection on Satisfaction

Stop and reflect on what your greatest moments of satisfaction have been. This is a little different from getting good news about something or having a great time. This is a deeper satisfaction, one of feeling really connected to the world. It is often accompanied by a sense of belonging. Take the time to reflect on and write down what these moments have been in your life. Go into detail about each one. Who was there? What were you thinking? What was the feeling like? See what this says about what is really important in life.

Respecting Others' Beliefs and Practices

If you get into a particular spiritual practice, you may have the desire to tell other people and try to get them to do it. This is common, but it can be a drag for your friends. Often we try to get someone to do a practice because we want reassurance that the practice is a good one. We want their approval, and our telling them about it is a way to get it.

While the desire may be great, it is usually good to resist telling other people about a practice until it has become rooted in yourself. Telling people about something is always hard because some things can not be expressed in words. Rather than trying to get other people to do something like meditate, focus on living what you learn from your practice. There is no way you can ever really *know* the truth, you can only live and be it. When something becomes a part of you, it is expressed not just in your words, but in your presence.

A meditation teacher once got a letter from a student who said that whenever she went home to visit her parents she always got into arguments with them about Buddhism and Christianity. Her parents were Christians and were concerned about her interest in Buddhism. However, they noticed positive changes in her. Over time she learned to just live and be the essence of the practice rather than argue about the different beliefs of the traditions. She later wrote, "My parents hate me when I am Buddhist, but they love me when I am the Buddha."

I think actually living the benefits is the real practice. In this sense, it does not matter whether one practices Buddhist meditation or Christian prayer or Hindu devotional chanting or nothing at all. What matters are the qualities of kindness, wisdom, and compassion that are nurtured and developed. Practices can change over time. One can be drawn to meditation for many years, then later develop an interest in prayer or something else. It is not the forms that matter so much, it is the formless ideas that underlie them. Certain qualities cannot be measured. We are the only person who knows whether something is helping us develop the qualities of the heart. We cannot lie or deceive our own heart. When a practice or teaching is right, even if it may seem strange or new, in our heart we know it. And if a practice or teaching does not feel right, even if it is comfortable and known, we know it as well. There is no deceiving the inner voice.

The Buddha at one point said that the purpose of practice was not to make one smarter or wiser, or to develop certain states of mind or even to be a better person. He said that while all these are important, the true purpose of practice is what he called "the sure heart's release." No tradition or system has the only key to the sure heart's release. It asks us to listen to and trust ourselves. While the desire to tell other people about a practice often comes from a good place, it is a real art to offer teachings without people feeling judged or "lectured to." What we can give to others is only what we have lived and experienced.

One time a woman came with her son to Gandhi and said to him, "My son is eating too much sugar and will not listen to me. Can you please tell him to not eat sugar anymore."

Gandhi replied, "Come back in two weeks." The woman was confused by this, but Gandhi was one of the greatest leaders in India and she was certainly not going to argue with him.

Two weeks later the child and mother returned. The mother repeated the problem and the boy walked up and knelt before Gandhi. Gandhi talked to the boy for a few minutes then said to him, "Please respect your mother's wishes. Don't eat sugar."

The boy nodded his head in agreement. As the mother was leaving, she turned to Gandhi and said, "Thank you very much, but I am wondering why you could not have said that two weeks ago when we visited."

"Two weeks ago," Gandhi said, "I was eating sugar."

We may have wonderful ideas, but it can be helpful to wait until those ideas are fully practiced and embodied before offering them to others. However, once we feel a practice is a part of us, it can be wonderful to share it with others. The practice is never "just for ourselves." There will be a time when we are ready to spread the practice to our community. As the practice becomes a part of us, we will feel easier about explaining it to others who are interested. While the words we choose are important, our presence will say as much as anything.

Creating Your Own Guide for a Healthy Lifestyle

Spiritual practice does not require that we take on a particular lifestyle per se; but as we learn to open our mind and heart, we notice that certain actions support our practice while others are a hindrance to it. You may find yourself limiting certain activities, such as the time you spend watching television. You do this not because you "should" but because you notice that after many hours of television it is very hard to think clearly. You may also start eating less, or going to sleep earlier, or gossiping about others less, or various other actions. As you become more sensitized to your body and mind, those changes in lifestyle that support awareness and compassion and those that take away from it become more evident.

It is important that these changes come from your direct experience. People telling you to do this or that or not do this or that may be helpful in getting you to check something out, but real change only comes from direct experience. When we are young, we have people telling us what to do all the time. Parents and teachers often have good intentions in giving us advice—they honestly believe that if we do a certain action (like meditate) it will ease some of our suffering. Sometimes they are right, sometimes not. However, another person's encouragement can only get us started. Without direct personal experience as to something's benefit, we cannot sustain our commitment.

We often think of refraining from certain actions, like getting wasted or high, as a surrender to a life of boredom. We now feel doomed to spend the rest of our life sitting at home missing out on everything fun. But there is a way that changes in lifestyle can add more richness to our life, not take it away. If we decide to drink less beer or none at all, it does not mean that we must surrender to a life of boredom in front of the television. Such changes should add more quality to our lives; they should give us more of a sense of mystery and adventure.

We all must see for ourselves what causes suffering and what brings more joy and happiness. There are many valuable books on the subject, but it still comes back to your own heart and mind. We can hear the most profound words from someone, but if we do not have the direct experience to relate it to, the words do not go far. Only by paying attention to life can we learn for ourselves.

Numerous spiritual traditions offer guidelines or precepts to follow. Traditionally, in Buddhism, there are five: not to kill, not to steal, not to create suffering through one's sexuality, not to speak untruthfully, and not to abuse intoxicants that cloud the mind. Often if one goes to a Buddhist monastery in Asia and asks to receive advanced meditation training, they begin by talking about the five precepts. Many centers feel that if one is not established in the five precepts, it is not useful to practice intensive meditation. They want there to be a strong foundation upon which to build.

The first precept, not killing, can be very challenging to practice. Some people who practice this precept become vegetarian to reduce the animal suffering that a meat-based diet supports. Others are very careful to carry spiders and other insects out of their house rather than immediately swat them. They are also careful not to step on insects while walking. This precept can be taken to various levels.

The second precept, not stealing, involves not taking what was not given. This, of course, means to not rob banks or steal cars, but at a deeper level it can also mean not living in a way that uses great amounts of resources at the expense of others.

The third precept is to be mindful of how one uses his or her sexual energy, and to not use it in ways that create suffering. This means being conscious of sexuality and seeing both the great love and the great pain it can cause.

The fourth precept, not lying, involves not speaking what we know is untrue or that we are unsure of. This can also include gossiping or talking behind someone's back.

The fifth precept is to avoid taking intoxicants that cause one to be careless or heedless. Some Buddhist traditions take this to mean not to use any alcohol or drugs, while others interpret it to mean that one can enjoy certain intoxicants as long as one does not use them to the degree that they limit mindfulness. But the basic idea is to be attentive to how one uses intoxicants.

Practicing the precepts can bring up many difficult questions with which to grapple. Even just practicing the first precept, not killing, can be very challenging. A few weeks ago I drove my car on a trip and noticed how many animals were killed on my windshield during the trip. Driving a car also creates air and water pollution that makes it harder for animals to survive. Do I need to give up driving my car to really practice the first precept, or is there another way to work with this?

There was a Vietnamese monk who burned himself to death to raise awareness to the horrors of the Vietnam war. Was he breaking the precept of not killing by killing himself, or was his death saving more lives by bringing more awareness to the war? If we see a deer run through the woods and a hunter comes by a few minutes later and asks us if we saw which way the deer went, do we lie and say we did not see it or do we speak the truth and endanger the life of the deer? Or do we say, "I know, but I won't tell you"?

I know no easy answers to these questions. Precepts can be important because in a moment of forgetfulness, they remind us of our intention. If we take the precept not to lie, then a few weeks later find ourselves about to tell a small lie to a friend to get out of an engagement, we then remember our previous intention, and we can explore how to relate to the situation in a more honest way. Or if we take on the precept not to kill, we might remember it as we lift our hand to swat a mosquito. We can then explore whether there is another way to deal with the situation other than killing. Sometimes our choices seem limited, but precepts can help us explore such situations rather than habitually act out old patterns that we may no longer wish to continue. But in reality, it is almost impossible to keep any code or precept completely. We can only do our best.

Just in driving my car, I know I cause harm to other life forms, but I try to do my best. At times during the year, I say an apology to all the beings that I caused harm to, either knowingly or unknowingly. We all cause a certain amount of suffering to other beings. We can use a vow or a precept to encourage us to do our best, even though we know that it may be impossible to actually live up to it.

Sometimes the precepts are referred to as mindfulness trainings. They are more like reminders or trainings that help us live more fully. The word *precepts* sometimes makes people think of rigid rules that they must follow. Seeing them as mindfulness trainings reminds us that it is a practice, that we try to follow such guidelines not because of some religious code or because we are bad if we do not, but simply to nurture our own practice and life. But it is also a form of social engagement. Living in a way that supports honesty, respect for others' belongings, non-killing, respect for sexuality, and attentiveness to intoxicants is also a form of creating the world we want.

So our work in the world becomes a part of our practice. Whether we are working to cultivate these qualities in ourselves or the world around us, it is the same work. Working to save trees or for social issues is simply an extension of the inner work that we do; it is not different from it. Precepts or guidelines then become a reminder to support that which is most precious to us, both in ourselves and the world.

Codes to Live By

Create your own list of "codes to live by." If you had to come up with a list of codes to live by, what would they be? What do you feel is important in life to remember? You will probably never be able to live according to this list one hundred percent of the time. It is more a guiding list, one that expresses your intention.

For example, one code may be "I vow to practice compassion." Now, no one (at least no one that I know) is compassionate all the time, but such a phrase can help you remember to do this more and more often. So this list is simply what you feel is important. It might be useful to go through and read the different precepts or codes of various religions or traditions. What have other people come up with? Then find what feels right for you. As you grow and change, so will this list, depending on what you feel is important at a particular time.

Loving Is Enough

Love is probably the most powerful human emotion. Any songwriter or poet can attest to this. It can be one of the most powerful experiences, but it can also be one of the most confusing. Many times love is confused with intimacy or sexual desire. We think if we are attracted to someone, we must love him or her. However, what we feel is often desire, not love. Of course the two can coexist, but they can also be confused, as most of us know. We often only realize this after we have received the person or object of our desire, and find that although we got what we wanted, love is nowhere to be found.

Talking about love can seem kind of silly. We might think, "How dumb. Just love people. Yeah, right." But think of the **233** times when you felt loved and cared for by someone, times you felt that someone was looking out for your interests. No matter how difficult your life may be, when someone honestly cares for you, you feel it. It is this feeling, call it love or care or whatever, that is so powerful, yet so elusive.

The Buddha said that hatred never ceases by hatred; hatred only ceases by love. We can start to practice this first with ourselves. Our hatred will never cease by beating ourselves up. It will only cease by treating ourselves with kindness, compassion, and forgiveness. Self-hatred makes us more hateful. Care for ourselves makes us more caring.

So it begins at home, which is something few of us have ever been taught. How many of us were ever taught to be kind to ourselves? We may have been told to be kind to a friend or a sibling, but few of us were ever taught the importance of self-kindness and care. There is no one to blame. We live in a culture where we are constantly encouraged to think we are not enough—not wealthy enough, not pretty enough, not smart enough, not successful enough. It is impossible for most of us to live up to the images of beauty and success that we see. Trying to live up to these ideals of perfection causes many people to become bulimic, spend thousands of dollars on clothes, or begin drugs like speed to lose every ounce of fat on their body. The images that we measure ourselves against can enslave us. We beat ourselves up every time we look in the mirror and do not look how we think we are supposed to look or every time we read about someone else who is more monetarily "successful" than we are. We tell ourselves over and over that who we are is not enough. So when we begin to send acceptance and care to ourselves, it feels a little strange. We think, "Who am I to deserve love? What did I ever do to deserve care and compassion?" This is the old conditioned mind trying to convince us that we are not enough, that we do not deserve care. But we do not have to "do" anything to deserve love. It is our birthright.

We have all had moments when we wished we were dead, when we wished we could just check out of life. I know no one who has not felt this at one time or another. If we reflect, we see that each of us has endured incredible hardship and pain. Rather than touch that pain with blame and guilt, we can begin to have compassion for ourselves, for this person we are who is doing his or her best, and who too wishes to be happy.

One of the main drugs of our culture is unworthiness. We believe that we aren't enough just as we are and need some product to be worthy—a certain kind of beer, a particular jacket, a new cologne. We look at ourselves through the eyes of unworthiness, through the eyes of not being enough. But when we look at ourselves through God's eyes or the eyes of some merciful being, which are the eyes of our deepest being, we see ourselves in a different light. We see that we are actually a precious creature. When we see ourselves through God's eyes, there is nothing to condemn or judge. We see that it is not in meeting some external image of success and beauty that brings happiness, but rather in bringing forth our own beauty—our joy, our laughter, our care. Greater than our longing to be someone else is the longing to be who we really are.

We can practice relating to ourselves from our heart rather than from external images. We can begin to open our heart to ourselves just as we are. Not who we can be or who we might be tomorrow or who we want to be, but who we are in this moment. Accepting all of our fear, anxiety, and pain; taking ourselves in our heart "as is," waiting for nothing to change. Love of ourselves can never wait for sometime later. Either it accepts us completely in this moment, including all of our joy and pain, or else it is not true love.

Once we have received care from ourselves then we can begin to extend it to others. Sometimes the only other being we love is a pet or a close friend. If we begin with that being and focus on developing our love for them, it will naturally extend to others. Trying to love the entire human race may be too much for many of us. Begin with developing your love for the people you do love, then gradually extend this to acquaintances, then to people you do not know, then gradually to people you dislike. This way, your love naturally builds from yourself, to your friends, and then out to others. When love for ourselves becomes the foundation, our heart has firm ground on which to build.

The Buddha put a great amount of focus on love. He said, "that which is most needed is a loving heart." He went on to say, "Just as the moon is sixteen times stronger than the light of all the stars, so is lovingkindness sixteen times more efficacious in liberating the heart than all other religious accomplishments taken together."

The emphasis on love can be found in numerous spiritual traditions. Mother Teresa writes, "The greatest disease in the West today is not TB or leprosy; it is being unwanted, unloved, and uncared for. We can cure physical diseases with medicine, but the only cure for loneliness, despair, and hopelessness is love. There are many in the world who are dying for a piece of bread but there are many more dying for a little love. The poverty in the West is a different kind of poverty—it is not only a poverty of loneliness but also of spirituality."

Love is so simple. We all have access to it. It is our natural state. Yet it is so easy to forget its importance. So much of the work is just about remembering.

Your Life Is Your Message

When many of us hear of generosity, we think of the act of giving a material object to another. While this is a part of generosity, there is also "generosity of spirit." Generosity is also a way of being, an attitude towards life in which one accepts and lets go freely.

Generosity is not just about giving money. You may not have money, but you might have time, or a certain skill that others could use; but most of all, you have your presence. When I hear people talk of influential teachers and mentors in their life, I hear them speak of the care and attention someone gave them. Rarely do I hear people talk about the expertise of a mentor or what they received

materially. Usually people talk about the acts that are hard to measure, the times this person listened to and supported them.

One of my greatest teachings on generosity came from a homeless child in Calcutta, India. Calcutta is a very poor city, and a good number of children are homeless. Many of these children beg on the streets in front of the hotels and guesthouses where foreigners stay. The sight of these children with bloated bellies wearing torn clothes running up to me asking for money was too much for me to take when I first arrived there, and I stayed in my guesthouse for several days, afraid to leave. A few days later, I cautiously stepped out of my guesthouse and turned the corner to find four or five children running toward me. I almost turned to go back inside when I made eye contact with one of the children. *This is just a child,* I thought to myself. Instead of turning away, I picked him up in my arms and held him. The kid warmed up to me quickly, he so craved contact of any kind. I soon became friends with these children and walked hand-in-hand with them around the city. They showed me where the post office was and where to buy train tickets. One day I was returning from the post office with one of the homeless kids when we stopped at a fruit stand. I bought a banana for me and one for him. I sat down to eat mine, but realized that the child had walked away. I was surprised he would leave without saying good-bye so I started to look for him. I peeked down an alley and knew immediately why he left in such a hurry. While I was eating my banana, he had rounded up four of his friends and was tearing the banana I gave him into five pieces, giving each one of his friends an equal piece. Imagine being hungry and poor, living on the streets, and as soon as you are given food, rather than quickly eating it, thinking of your friends who are hungry and sharing it with them. I marveled at the level of compassion and generosity of this child! He was the poorest of the poor living on the streets of Calcutta, yet his heart was as wide as the world. He gave me a whole new under-standing of the word generosity. He had so little, yet what he received he shared openly.

This does not mean that wealthy people are somehow less generous, but that generosity is not just about money. It is a quality that involves seeing that the nature of life is change, and that when it comes down to it, we really do not own anything. Everything belongs to the earth and will return to the earth, even our bodies. Knowing this, we put less importance on the objects in our life. We still need a house and clothes, but we are simply the current renters of all that we own. We cannot bring any of it with us when we pass away.

Knowing this helps us practice wisdom and generosity by giving to others materially and also in spirit. Jesus said if someone asks for your coat you should give them the shirt off your back. Buddha said that if you knew what he knew about generosity, you would give away a part of every meal. While these are lovely ideals, most of us are not there yet. When giving feels like it is forced and we push ourselves, thinking we "should" be generous, we only get resentful. Generosity must come from a full heart, not a heart that is lacking. Just as with lovingkindness, we should not forget to be generous to ourselves. This means not only giving ourselves our kindness and care, but also giving ourselves time to be in the woods or to listen to music or to do other things that we enjoy.

Generosity is an openness of being, a willingness to receive and let go, an understanding of the nature of life. This generosity of spirit is represented in a story of Gandhi. Once Gandhi was boarding a train while traveling in India and was approached by someone from his home district and asked if he had a message to send back home. He was boarding the train and did not have much time. He grabbed a paper bag, wrote something, and handed it to the person. It read, "My life is my message." That's generosity of spirit. For Gandhi, every act was a practice in generosity. His entire life was his offering; his entire life was his gift.

Mother Teresa reminds us that we all have something to give, and that it is simple human contact that often has the most impact. She writes, "Charity and love are the same—with charity you give love, so don't just give money but reach out your hand instead. When I was in London, I went to see the homeless people where our sisters have a soup kitchen. One man, who was living in a cardboard box, held my hand and said, 'It has been a long time since I have felt the warmth of a human hand.'"

A human hand or a caring smile is something we can all give. We don't need money or special training for this. All we need is true presence, which is always within us and can never run out. This is the giving that replenishes when it is given.

There Are Forces Stronger Than Any Machine

Have you ever noticed that when someone is mean or uncool to you, you want to treat them back the same way—or worse? I certainly do at times. When someone causes us pain or discomfort, our initial response is to return the pain in any way possible. In moments of pain, there is a strong desire to attempt to heal that pain by making someone else feel like we feel. However, this reaction makes the pain never-ending. While this cycle is understandable, the more we continue it, the more it comes back to ourselves. Numerous activists in history have revealed to us that we can learn to relate to pain and suffering in a way that does not perpetuate it. Otherwise, we are just passing it along. As Gandhi said, "An eye for

243

an eye only makes the whole world blind." Jesus put it another way: "You have heard that it was said, 'An eye for an eye, and a tooth for a tooth.' But I say unto you, do not resist him who is evil but whoever slaps you on the right cheek, turn to him the other also."

You might be thinking, "Yeah, right. I'd like to see Gandhi or Jesus try that in *my* neighborhood." Giving someone our other cheek when hit is really an ideal. We might need to begin by simply not hitting someone when they insult us, or learning to walk away, or screaming and yelling in frustration but not acting out in violence. Though ideally we would offer the other cheek, it is easier said than done. Most importantly, we need to take steps in the right direction.

I think we at times need to respond to the anger and cruelty that comes our way; but there is a way of responding that makes the conflict worse and one that makes reconciliation more likely. I'm not saying this is easy and I'm not saying that I can do it all the time, I'm just saying that there are more creative ways to respond than to meet meanness with more meanness.

A commitment to not passing on suffering does not mean that we open ourselves to needless pain or do not respect and stand up for our rights. It's just the opposite. A commitment to heal suffering is an active, not a passive,

Just Say OM!

244

act. We become committed to responding to suffering in others and ourselves in ways that truly heal.

For Gandhi, the commitment to nonviolence was anything but a passive act. His nonviolence was not a surrender; it was not a lack of action. He writes, "My *ahimsa* (nonviolence) is neither maimed nor weak. It is all-powerful. Where there is *ahimsa*, there is Truth, and Truth is God." Gandhi's nonviolence was based on strength—not the strength of armies or machines, but the strength of the human spirit. It was based on the limitless strength of the human heart. He was not trying to dominate or destroy, but to stand up for the rights of Indians in a way that did not cause any harm to the British. He demanded that the British leave India, but said that they must leave as friends.

There are situations that seem to question whether a use of violence actually creates less violence in the end—using violence to overthrow a dictator who is harming his own and other people, using it to stop someone who is going to do harm, or using violence to prevent the destruction of countless trees and wildlife. There are no easy answers to any of these situations, for every situation is unique. While there seem to be some useful examples of this working in history, countless other times we have seen violence used in the name of God or religion or liberty that has produced more deaths and enormous suffering for

245

thousands of people. People thought they were fighting a "just" war only to realize that they soon became the very thing that they were fighting against. They had become like their enemy in order to defeat them, and once they achieved power nothing much really changed, for the path they took to get there made them no different than those before them.

Whatever action one decides to take in a given situation, I think it is not only the action, but the spirit of the action that is important. One can act in a strong and powerful way to defend a loved one or to prevent harm without breeding more hatred in one's heart and encouraging the chain of suffering. Actions can be taken with an open heart, with a spirit that does not separate the world into the "good" and "bad" and the "right" and "wrong," or into those on God's side and those who are not.

Numerous martial arts practice ways of blending with or deflecting aggression to protect oneself and others. The martial art Aikido uses the energy of the attacker to subdue him in a way that causes no harm to your attacker while protecting yourself. Morihei Uyeshiba, the founder of the martial art Aikido, looked at the issue of nonviolence from this deep perspective. He said, "When an enemy tries to fight with me, the universe itself, he has to break the energy of the universe. Hence, at that moment he has the mind to fight with me, he is already defeated." By identifying with the energy of the universe, the battle is not just between two people. Rather it is a question of alignment, of being in harmony with the natural way of things.

Rickson Gracie, the Brazilian jiu-jitsu champion and arguably one the world's greatest martial artists, takes a similar approach to martial arts. He says that *ahimsa* or nonviolence is also the founding principle of his jiu-jitsu, which he dates back 4,000 years to Hindu ascetics. He has said that the true powers in life are not in external strength but are the powers of "kindness, smiling, and flexibility." The message from great martial artists and social activists is the same: that the real work is in using the external challenges as a way to understand ourselves better. It is learning to deal with our own emotions and feelings so as to create less suffering in the world.

Right action is an important part of spiritual practice. A spiritual life does not mean that one is no longer involved in the world. The question is not so much *whether* we act, but *how* we act. Even not getting involved is an action. Those who see spiritual practice as a type of nonaction are not looking deeply enough. Thich Nhat Hanh writes, "Nonviolence does not mean nonaction. Nonviolence means that we *act* with love and compassion. The moment we stop acting we undermine the principle of nonviolence."

Nonviolence is not a weakness but is possibly the greatest strength that exists. The amount of violence we see in our society is a sign of how isolated we have become. Neighborhoods are not safe to walk through, and many people walk around on guard, watching for the possible attacker. While this is understandable, a spiritual practice must address the issue of violence and strive to bring forth greater respect and reverence for life. Any practice must step out and address the larger society. The world we see becomes a part of our practice, both the beautiful and the not-so-beautiful parts of it.

Some of the greatest activists in our time are characterized by their dedication to nonviolence. We have numerous examples of people who relied on this greater force of nonviolence to win a battle. Martin Luther King Jr. spoke of using the suffering inflicted by another to gain more strength and eventually win them over. He talked about meeting physical force with "soul force."

The soul force to which Dr. King speaks is stronger than any weapon that can be created. Though we might not know what the "right" action is in a given moment, the more we ask the question and listen, the more guidance we will receive.

Everyone Has Something to Give

The question of how to help others is an important one. We all know how it feels when someone thinks they are helping us but really they are not. There is a story of a Native American boy who came to the white man's city for the first time. He had never seen large buildings before, and he was awed by the large doors and architecture. He wondered what it would be like to open a large door to one of the buildings. He decided to give it a try. The door was heavier than he thought, and he had to struggle with it. As he tried to open it, a white man came up and pushed the door open, thinking that he was helping. The Indian boy got upset with him because the man had ruined his experience of opening the door.

What actually helps is not so obvious. The writer and teacher Ram Dass talks about being in an environment where suffering can be seen and let go of without force. He writes, "To the extent we ourselves are free from suffering, our very being becomes an environment in which others can be free of theirs, if it is in the way of things." How do we become an environment that does not attempt to force change, but where there is nothing in us that is supporting the continuation of suffering? When we try to force others to change, it is we who need help with our suffering. So how do we balance the natural caring of our heart to relieve suffering, with equanimity, trust, and non-force?

We all have our idea of how the world would be if we were in charge. When I was in my early twenties I was very involved in the rising environmental movement at that time. More people were beginning to see the destructiveness of mainstream consumer society and the desperate need to change our ways. Many of my friends and I were determined to make it all better, now! We despised cars, and tried to walk or hitchhike instead. I would not eat in restaurants because I thought everyone should be growing their own food, and I did not want to support any industry that disconnected a person from the land. We disagreed with most of the modern culture and vowed to not be a part of it. I hated people who did not see everything as I saw it. I had no patience for people who ate meat or who made a lot of money or who thought that everything was fine in the world. We felt that there was this group of "us," who were trying to save the earth, and this "them," who were destroying it. If only "they" would listen to "us" then everything would be fine. They probably thought the same way: the world would be better if only we would listen to them.

While our ideals were for the most part genuine, they were not based on trust and belief in people. We were against much, but for little. We wanted to help, but knew no other way of helping than to divide ourselves from others and believe others to be the enemy. However, I think the genuine desire to help the world and to live in balance with nature is a profound longing. The question seems to be how to act in a way that truly helps, that does not breed more anger and hatred in the name of doing good.

I don't think there are any set answers to this question, but I believe that the process asks us to trust ourselves. It asks us to explore our own heart. One great Indian teacher said, "Never put anyone out of your heart." I try to remember this when I am questioning an action. In this action am I putting someone out of my heart, or am I making more room in my heart for myself and others?

Many people think they have nothing to give. They are not masters in any art nor do they feel they have any special knowledge to espouse. However, each of us has something to give. It may be that we feed people who are hungry or hold the hand of someone who is dying or talk to a homeless person. This is not the kind of service that thinks *I'm giving you something, so you must give me something in return.* Rather, as we open our mind and heart we are naturally pulled to do what we can to relieve suffering in the world. When we see a need, we are naturally pulled to help.

A sense of service can come through in small ways. For example, we can take on the practice of always saying hello to the mailman or we can practice actually seeing the cashier when we purchase something. Rather than think we need to go off to Asia or Africa to do service work or think we need to take on some grand project, we can bring an attitude of service into our everyday actions. Making contact and really seeing the person at the checkout stand or the mailman becomes a part of our practice.

When I worked as a cashier at a deli, numerous people passed through each day, but few would ever make real contact with me. I wondered how I might connect with them more. After people ordered, while they were waiting for me to ring up their total, I began asking each person what their favorite quote was. I told them that I was collecting the Quote of the Day and would tell them the winner the following day. Some people ignored me and did not respond, but the vast majority lit up like a candle and uttered inspiring phrases from Jesus or the poet Rilke or the Native American tradition. I was amazed at what people came up with on the spot. So many people had beautiful quotes to share. Soon I had people calling me at work telling me other quotes that they liked and coming into the store for no other reason than to hand me some quote they had just read. It was a wonderful event. The atmosphere in the deli changed into a true learning environment. My manager was not sure what to make of this, but she could not say much about it since clearly our customers were happier.

For almost a year, I saw this as my main service work: to help people remember sayings that inspired them, to help myself and others remember what is meaningful. It soon changed my somewhat monotonous job into a day of spiritual teachings. The people who had previously not even acknowledged me were now offering me wonderful teachings each day. I don't know who benefited more from this event—me or the customers. Everyone who was willing to participate seemed nurtured by it.

The purpose of service is not to lift ourselves above others, thinking that we are such a good person, while subtly thinking that others are less than we are. This motivation to look good rather than do good is in all of us. While involved in work for the environment, many of us would half-jokingly say that more than wanting to help the planet, we wanted to be *seen* helping the planet. We would pick up a can and recycle it if there was a crowd around, but otherwise, forget it. This is in all of us. There is a part of us that wants to be seen as an earth-saver more than actually do the work. This need not prevent us from doing service work but simply reveal to us the great conditioning of the mind. While the desire to look good is in us, we each have much deeper motivations that can come forth.

A sense of service reminds us of our interconnectedness. It creates more unity and less division. The practice of service is ultimately to go beyond the ideas of service, the ideas of me helping you or you helping me, and to touch the underlying interconnectedness of which we are all a part.

The Great Mystery Is Here for Us All

All the great spiritual traditions tell us that no matter who you are, you can live a spiritual life. You do not need to have a certain education, or look a certain way, or have read particular books. It does not matter whether your parents were saints or whether they were cruel and uncaring. No matter if you have lived a mean and thoughtless life until now or a very caring one, everyone has the opportunity to take a path with heart, to live with care and respect. A true spiritual path does not exclude or condemn. It only asks that we bring our full heart and mind into life, that we be willing to see beauty and open our hearts even in the most difficult situations.

255

The spiritual path is a mysterious one, and far more challenging than any other endeavor. Our culture today focuses much more on our technological abilities and gives little attention to the spiritual aspects of life. But the spiritual path is as alive today as it ever has been.

One thing is certain, we never walk the path alone. Though it is up to each of us to do the work, we are joined on the path by all the great mystics and teachers of the ages who too have asked these questions. We carry the power of our parents, ancestors, and friends with us; and we carry the support of all those who have asked similar questions. We must do the work, but we have a great supporting cast. We never walk alone.

It takes courage to follow a path that feels genuine, that is aligned with our heart. Sometimes we have very little support and making the decisions to follow our heart takes great courage. The Christian mystic Thomas Merton once told fellow mystic Brother David Steindl-Rast, "You must have the courage to do the opposite of everyone else." I have always loved this line. He did not say that one *must* do the opposite of everyone else, only that the courage to do so be there, and the intention to follow it if and when the time comes. At some point in our life, though most people around us will be telling us something different, our heart will pull us in a particular direction.

Trusting this is no easy task, but not trusting it is even harder.

The spiritual journey is mysterious, and no one I know has it "all figured out." Our heart, strangely enough, seems to know the way. It asks us to go forth on a great journey of discovery. The meditation teacher and author Jack Kornfield writes, "Spiritual practice is revolutionary. It allows us to step outside our personal identity, culture, and religion to experience more directly the great mystery, the great music of life."

This great music plays through all the great traditions. There is no perfect religion or spiritual practice. Maybe if someone knitted or skateboarded every day with their full attention they would get the same insights as meditation or prayer. Who knows? And every practice and tradition has its shortcomings. Buddhism is certainly not the perfect tradition. Several countries where Buddhism is practiced in great number have in recent years been torn by war or dictatorship. Every tradition and practice has its shortcomings. In our culture today we seem to be developing and adapting ancient forms to have relevance in our contemporary world. The great music of life still plays, as it has since the beginning. We each dance to its tune in our own way, but we are all dancers. We are all voyagers in the life process. We may not be the most eloquent or talented dancer, but we each have the opportunity to leave our own mark and to make the best of this life, however wacky and wild it can seem at times.

When the Buddha was dying and his students asked him for final guidance, he told them to be "lamps unto themselves" and to trust in the truth. He said that though he was dying, the truth would live on, forever. He basically encouraged them to trust themselves and told them that the truth should be their guide. This truth may not be something we can explain or describe, but we all know it when we see it, and we each have the ability to live in harmony with it.

Resource List

This book was meant to be an introduction to both meditation and wisdom stories and teachings. There are many wonderful books that more thoroughly explore the subjects addressed here. The following list is not meant to be The Ultimate List of books on this subject, but rather a beginning for further research. Clearly, books are like candy. Everyone has their own tastes. I have found my favorite books by word of mouth and from looking at the suggested reading lists in the back of books that I enjoyed.

Mindfulness and the Spiritual Path

If you are interested in the practice of meditation and mindfulness, a very good book is *Wherever You Go, There You Are* by Jon Kabat-Zinn. This book offers an in-depth discussion of mindfulness. It is more in the tradition of people like Henry David Thoreau and others who attempted to live fully, rather than a Buddhist meditation book. For a book that integrates Buddhism, meditation, and psychotherapy, Jack Kornfield's *A Path With Heart* is an excellent read. A former Buddhist monk and practicing psychotherapist, the author shows the benefits of both these traditions, weaving in many great stories and quotes along the way.

In this same spirit, I have loved the work of Bo Lozoff who writes both for the general public and for people doing spiritual practice while incarcerated. Two of my favorites are *Lineage*, a series of short stories, and *Deep and Simple*. These books are mainly sold through the Human Kindness Foundation, so if you want a catalog, write to the foundation at Route 1, Box 201-N, Durham, NC 27705.

Buddhist Meditation

Insight Meditation

There are many books on insight meditation, the first meditation discussed in this book. Books by Joseph Goldstein include *The Experience of Insight, Insight Meditation,* and *Seeking the Heart of Wisdom* (with Jack Kornfield). All explain the basics of insight meditation and this teacher's work over many years of experience. A book on starting a meditation practice is Stephen Levine's *A Gradual Awakening.* A more traditional view of insight meditation can be found in *The Heart of Buddhist Meditation* by Nyanaponika Thera, which goes through and describes various Buddhist meditations and the differences between them. For a book on more heart-centered meditation practice in this tradition, please consult *Lovingkindness: The Revolutionary Art of Happiness* by Sharon Salzberg.

Tibetan Buddhist Meditation

All books by the Dalai Lama, the spiritual leader of Tibet, are great. I have particularly enjoyed the recent *The Art of Happiness.* Another book on Tibetan Buddhist teachings and meditation is *Awakening the Buddha Within* by Lama Surya Das, a high-ranking American Lama in the Tibetan Buddhist tradition. The book is very accessible and full of great information.

Other books on Tibetan Buddhism include Pema Chodron's *Wisdom of No Escape, Start Where You Are,* and *When Things Fall Apart.* These are all fairly easy-to-read teachings from an American woman's experience with Tibetan Buddhism. They are very applicable to ordinary life and the struggles we all face.

Zen Meditation

Books on Zen meditation practice include *Zen Mind, Beginner's Mind* by Suzuki Roshi from the Japanese Zen tradition, which is a classic in the field and one of the most widely read books on Zen meditation. This book was taken from talks given to students, and the depth of understanding of this wise teacher comes through very clearly. *Peace Is Every Step* and *The Miracle of Mindfulness* by Thich Nhat Hanh are excellent, practical books on meditation from the Vietnamese Zen tradition.

Christian Contemplative Practice

Gratefulness, the Heart of Prayer by Brother David Steindl-Rast is a particularly sweet look at the focus of mindfulness in the practice of prayer within the Christian tradition. Also, Mother Teresa's books, especially *A Simple Path*, are great books on the heart of contemplation and service work in the Christian tradition.

Engaged Spiritual Practice

Books on service work and helping include two books by Ram Dass: *How Can I Help?* (with Paul Gorman) and *The Compassionate Heart* (with Mirabai Bush). They are great books on the joys and difficulties of trying to reach out. *Bearing Witness* by Roshi Bernard Glassman is a Zen teacher's views and experiences of socially engaged work.

Books for Young Adults

Ophelia Speaks, edited by Sara Shandler, is a wonderful collection of writings by teenage girls. The pieces are honest, straightforward, and real. *Chicken Soup for the Teenage Soul* and

Chicken Soup for the College Soul are both more inspirational and humorous collections of writings about the teenage and college years. Another book directed toward this population is *Meetings with Mentors* by a guy named Soren Gordhamer. It is a series of interviews with philosophers, psychologists, environmentalists, and spiritual teachers on the relationship between youth and elders in our society. The author's mother really liked it.

Poetry

My favorite has to be *The Kabir Book* versions by Robert Bly, which is a passionate display of the intensity of the spiritual quest. Also, the poetry of the Persian poet Rumi is extremely inspirational. There are numerous translations of his work. One, titled *Open Secret,* is a classic. The poetry of Emerson and Walt Whitman are also full of great insight. A good collection of spiritual poetry throughout the world is *The Enlightened Heart* compiled by Stephen Mitchell.

Books on the Spiritual Journey

There are many great books that speak of the incredible mystical journey of life. Two of my favorites are *Of Water and the Spirit* by the African shaman Malidoma Somé and *The Way of the Peaceful Warrior* by Dan Millman. The former is the incredible story of a young African man who is taken away from his village in Africa and later returns to learn the wisdom of the elders and the tribe. *The Way of the Peaceful Warrior* is a story about a man's search for happiness, and his meeting with a wise mentor who helps show him the way.

Index

Index

265

About the Author

Soren Gordhamer has been teaching meditation to teens for the past six years in such places as Spirit Rock Meditation Center, hospitals, drug treatment centers, camps, juvenile halls, and youth prisons. He is cofounder and executive director of The Lineage Project, a nonprofit organization that teaches meditation and yoga to at-risk and incarcerated teens in New York City. The organization recently won the Mayor's Voluntary Action Award for its work. Soren currently teaches classes for teens in the New York City area, where he lives with his partner, Maile Pickett, and their two dogs. In his free time, he enjoys traveling and going on hikes with his dogs. He is also the author of the book of interviews entitled *Meeting with Mentors: A Young Adult Interviews Leading Visionaries* (Hanford Mead Publishers, 1995).

The Lineage Project can be reached at:
PO Box 366, Mt. Vernon, NY 10552
www.lineageproject.com
Lineagepro@aol.com